JAI HIND

THE STORY OF LT. RAMA KHANDWALA OF NETAJI SUBHAS CHANDRA BOSE AZAD HIND FAUJ

RAMA KHANDWALA

MOT-MOT PUBLISHING

ISBN: 978-0-9979415-7-9

Photos: Rama Khandwala, Bina Cline, Public Domain. Photo of Rama Khandwala
receiving national tourism award courtesy of President of India Facebook page.

Cover: Vakils, Feffer & Simons Pvt. Ltd.

❀ Created with Vellum

Dedicated to my paternal grandfather
Dr. Pranjian Jagjivan Mehta
Gandhiji's greatest friend and benefactor
'I had no greater friend than Doctor Mehta in this whole world ...'
Gandhi to Manilal R. Jhaveri, 4 August 1932

* * *

This book has been inspired by my beloved daughter Bina Cline, who has been and continues to be very loving, caring and concerned.
I wish her, my son-in-law, Kenneth Cline, and granddaughter, Nikki Elmore (nee Cline), lots of prosperity, success, good health and all the happiness in the world

FOREWORD

As Rama Khandwala's daughter, I was very proud when she published her book, *Jai Hind*, in 2017. There are not too many people who can write and publish a book at age 90! I know that for her it was a labor of love — as well as a demonstration of her love for India.

However, the book was only available in a limited print edition inside India. My husband, Ken, and I wondered if we could make an edition accessible to Indians around the world. During a trip to Mumbai in January 2019 to see my mother, we visited Mr. Arun K. Mehta, whose company, Vakils, Feffer & Simons Pvt. Ltd., had published my mother's book.

It so happens that Arunbhai is a distant cousin of mine via his family connection (great grand nephew) to Dr. Pranjivan Jagjivan Mehta, my mother's grandfather, who was famous for having supported Mahatma Gandhi in his freedom struggles. Arunbhai had published a biography of Dr. Mehta by S.R. Mehrotra, in 2014. He subsequently encouraged my mother to write about her own participation in the Indian freedom struggle. Arunbhai told her, as she explains in her own introduction to this book, "You write your story and I will publish it."

When we met with him, Arunbhai noted, with a smile, "I helped make your mother famous." He may be on to something as it was after her book was published that she was interviewed by newspapers, invited to give a TED talk and even had a film documentary made about her.

Ken and I then asked Arunbhai if he had any objection to us re-publishing my mother's book for the international market. We thought it would be particularly helpful to make an e-book version available on Amazon. Arunbhai responded that he had no objection at all — that, in fact, he would would be delighted to see my mother's story distributed more widely. He even sent us his files from the original edition that we modified to present in the format you see here. Without his help, we wouldn't have been able to publish this version so quickly.

So, again, I cannot thank Arunbhai enough for his extraordinary kindness and generosity in helping present my mother's story to the world — both in the original edition and now in this Amazon version!

The current text is essentially as published by Vakils, Feffer & Simons in 2017, except for a few grammatical adjustments, the addition of some photographs in my personal possession, a reorganization of the background material related to the death of Subhas Chandra Bose and the addition of footnotes to lend historical perspective. Our intention is to enable my mother to tell her story as she wrote it.

And what a story it is, as you will see! As a lieutenant in the Rani Jhansi Regiment of the Indian National Army during World War II, Rama Khandwala nee Mehta fought on the front lines of India's struggle for independence. I am very proud of her for serving her country in this manner and I hope that Indian readers of this book will feel the same.

Jai Hind!

Bina Cline,

Atlanta, Ga., U.S.A., April 2020

Rama Khandwala (center) with daughter Bina Cline (left) and granddaughter Nikki Elmore (right). Mumbai, January 2018.

ACKNOWLEDGMENTS

As a young recruit in the Azad Hind Fauj (Indian National Army), I did not understand that I was an important character in India's freedom struggle and was making history. Now that there is an interest in Netaji Subhas Chandra Bose's life, work and death, I decided to tell his story in brief, combined with my own small contribution, as a way to remind people of his fight against a power (Great Britain) that ruled a major part of the world at that time.

Subhas Chandra Bose.

In this book, I have tried my best to highlight Netaji's ideas, ideologies and principles, co-ordinating with his activities, speeches and writings. I have also endeavored to portray the human aspect of his life, including his secret marriage to Emilie Schenkl and his love letters to her. I have utilized much information from Vol. 7 of the *Netaji Research Bureau* publications.

I express my deep sense of gratitude and special thanks to Shri Arun Mehta of the publishing company Vakils, Feffer & Simons Pvt. Ltd., who helped, guided and inspired me to write this book.

I also would like to thank the late Shri Aba Sahib Raut for obtaining some photographs of the Rani Jhansi Regiment for me.

I shall always remain grateful to the late the Capt. Lakshmi Sehgal for her kindness, helpfulness and supportiveness all through the years I have known her.

Rama with Col. Lakshmi Sehgal in Kanpur at the latter's residence in January 1988.

The late Lt. Manwati Arya has also helped me and guided me throughout the period of our friendship.

My special thanks go out to Dr. Swarna D. Shah for her support and encouragement to write this book, without which I would never have put pen to paper. I wish her and her family lots of prosperity, success, happiness and good health.

Rama with best friend Swarna Shah at the latter's residence in Atlanta, U.S.A.

And I am grateful and thankful to Miss Jerroo Bharrucha, President of Tourist Guides Association (TOGA), Mumbai, for providing final touches and suggestions for this book.

INTRODUCTION

I was inspired to write this book on 7th March, 2014, when I attended a function for the release of the book *Mahatma and the Doctor* written by S.R. Mehrotra, about the friendship between Mahatma Gandhi and my grandfather, Dr. Pranjivan Jagjivan Mehta. The book was published by Mr. Arun Mehta of Vakils, Feffer and Simons Pvt. Ltd.

When he heard that I had been a freedom fighter during World War II, Arunbhai said to me, "You write your story and I will publish it."

I was born on December 3, 1926, in Rangoon (Yangon) Burma (Myanmar) to the very rich, famous, illustrious and patriotic family of Dr. Pranjivan Jagjivan Mehta. My father, Shri Chhaganlal Pranjivan Mehta, was the eldest son of Pranjivanbhai. I was the fifth child in the family, which comprised four girls and three boys.

At that time, Burma was part of India and likewise under British rule.[1] As a result, there were a lot of Indian settlers in Burma. My father was in the jewelry business, and owned a shop at 121 Mogul Street, Rangoon.[2] I remember a dosa (rice pancake) shop nearby where we used to eat onion dosas. We went to a private school, Diocesan Girls High School, where we were repeatedly told that "Britain shall always rule the waves."[3]

Rama at age 16 in Rangoon before the war.

When Japan entered the Second World War in December 1941, everything changed. The British government had to leave and the Japanese army conquered Rangoon in March 1942. We Indians welcomed the change in the government, believing that the new rulers, being Asian, were closer to us in culture. As the Japanese planes started bombing Rangoon, there was a lot of confusion and chaos among the Indians. Many of them started leaving to go to India. They walked with a few of their belongings and many died on the way. There was untold suffering. My family decided to stay in Rangoon, hence we were there during the entire war.

Rama with her mother, Lilavati Chhaganlal Mehta, in Burma just after the war.

The Japanese bombed Rangoon at the start of the war. Then after the British left, their planes returned to bomb Rangoon and other parts of Burma. We lived in the Jubilee Hall area, about a kilometer away from the anti-aircraft installations.[4] So, we were in part protected from the bombing but also partially at risk because the enemy would target those anti-aircraft installations. Their pilots preferred moonlit nights, as they could see the targets much better. At those times, the bombings would continue all night and we had to spend most of the time in trenches. We used to curse the moonlight.

As soon as the enemy planes came over, the siren would go on, warning us to get into our trenches. After the air raid was over, the clear siren would sound and we could resume our normal activities.

Most of the time, after the air raid was over, my elder brother and I would go to the bombing site. Needless to say, these experiences were beyond one's imagination and endurance. We would see dead bodies lying all over. Some were buried under the debris of the crushed buildings, some with no arms or legs. We saw children orphaned and crying. We would help in whatever way we could and I would always pray that there would be no more wars and such suffering in the world.

---

1. After three Anglo-Burma Wars (1825, 1852 and 1885) Burma was conquered and transformed into a British colony. Burma became an official colony on January 1, 1886. The British ruled Burma as a part of India from 1919 until 1937, when Burma was made a crown colony of Britain.
2. Mogul Street, now Shwe Bon Thar Road, was the heart of the traditionally Indian section of Rangoon before the war. The district is still home to lots of jewelry shops.
3. The high school mentioned is most likely St. Mary's Diocesan Girls High School, which was founded in 1866 and still in use today, albeit under a different name. See https://www.yangonheritagetrust.org/formerly-st-mary-girls-school-received-a-blue-plaque.
4. Jubilee Hall was a public events building erected in Rangoon in 1898. See https://www.irrawaddy.com/specials/places-in-history/jubilee-hall-colonial-social-hub-hotbed-myanmar-independence-activity.html. The old Jubilee Hall was demolished in 1985. The site is currently being developed for a $300 million hotel and mixed use project. Rama's family lived in a house on Shwedagon Pagoda Road just opposite the old Jubilee Hall.

IMPORTANT DATES

- December 7, 1941: Japanese attack Pearl Harbor, Pacific War begins
- February 15, 1942: Singapore falls to the Japanese
- June 24, 1942: Indian Independence League (ILL) established in Bangkok
- July 4, 1943: Shri Subhas Chandra Bose becomes president of the ILL
- July 5, 1943: Formation of Azad Hind Fauj announced to the world
- August 25, 1943: Bose made Commander-in-Chief of the Fauj
- October 22, 1943: Rani Jhansi Regiment Camp inaugurated
- October 25, 1943: Azad Hind declares war on the British Empire and the U.S.A.
- November 8, 1943: Andaman and Nicobar islands transferred by Japanese to Azad Hind government
- December 30, 1943: Indian tricolor hoisted at Port Blair, capital of Andaman and Nicobar Islands

- March 18, 1944: Fauj Crosses into India (Imphal Campaign)
- March 22, 1944: Gen. Chatterjee becomes first governor of Liberated Areas in India
- July 20, 1944: Japanese give up Imphal attack and retreat back to Burma
- August 24, 1944: Military operations suspended due to monsoon
- April 24, 1945: Azad Hind Government leaves Rangoon for Bangkok
- May 3, 1945: Fauj surrenders Rangoon to the British

THE GREAT ESCAPE! THE DAWN OF
AZAD HIND FAUJ

❧

*N*etaji Subhas Chandra Bose resigned as president of the Congress Party on April 29, 1939, as desired by Mahatma Gandhi due to the ideological and tactical discordance between the two men. He started working intensively from the platform of his newly formed Congress wing, the All India Forward Bloc.[1] This made him more popular than he had been as president of the Congress party.

Netaji Subhas Chandra Bose as young man.

The All India Congress Committee, under the direction of Gandhiji, was alarmed to see Subhas Chandra Bose continue in power as the president of the Bengal Provincial Congress Committee.[2] They passed a resolution on August 19, 1939,

1

disqualifying him as the president of the B.P.C.C. on the grounds of deliberate and flagrant breach of discipline for three years. It made no difference to Subhas Chandra Bose. Due to his sincere and dedicated work and impressive speeches, he was popular with a mass following.

The world war broke out in the beginning of September 1939, as had been predicted by him in the past. It was detrimental for him to carry on his work and take full advantage of the conditions prevailing due to the war while being in conflict with the Indian National Congress. Unity in action is an indispensable factor for achieving success, which he proved later in the Indian National Army (INA). This ultimately impressed Gandhiji, leading him to praise Bose, who had given him the most honorable appellation as "Father of the Nation."

So while intensifying his work on the home front in India from the platform of the Forward Bloc, Subhas Chandra Bose started exploring the possibility of fleeing India incognito and opening a "second front" from outside India. He wanted his country to benefit from the experiences of other leaders that achieved independence by fleeing their homeland to seek help from countries belligerent to the common enemy.

Netaji Subhas Chandra Bose at his desk.

The old revolutionary, Rash Behari Bose, a political self-exile in Japan since 1915, had been working from that country in his efforts for Indian independence.[3] He had sent a letter to Subhas Chandra Bose in 1938 pleading with him to intensify organized violent struggles in India in view of the impending world war. But the British government intercepted the letter.

On the other hand, early in the summer of 1940, Subhas Chandra Bose had sent Shankerlal, General Secretary of the All India Forward Bloc, who was originally a rich business man and financial backer of Subhas Chandra Bose, to Japan to meet Rash Behari Bose and the Japanese Minister of Foreign Affairs, as well as the representatives of the German, Italian and Russian Governments.

The objective of the visit was to secretly explore a location where a second front of the war for Indian Independence could be opened. Subhas Chandra Bose also established contacts to plan his secret exit from India by traveling through the tribal hill areas of the North West Frontier Province and the area from Afghanistan to Russia, from where he expected to find help in his work.

On June 18, 1940, at the second All India Conference of Forward Bloc, Subhas Chandra Bose proclaimed, "It is for the Indian people to make an immediate demand for the transference of power through a provisional national government. When things have settled down inside India and abroad, the provisional national government will convene a constitutional assembly for framing a full-fledged Constitution for the country." He met Gandhiji for the last time after the Nagpur conference and returned to Calcutta after his failure to forge unity with him.

In Calcutta, he declared his intention to observe Sirajuddaula Day on July 1, 1940, and lead a procession demanding the demolition of the Howell Memorial Monument, knowing the ultimate result would be to divert the attention of the Government from his preparedness to flee.[4] On July 2, a day before Sirajuddaula Day, the British arrested him and sent him to jail for an indefinite period of detention. In jail, Subhas Chandra Bose planned his "great adventure" of escape through Afghanistan.

In the meantime, Shankar Zal, his emissary to Japan, returned by the end of June with encouraging information. But Shankar Zal could not get access to meet Bose personally in jail, so he sent the good tidings in code language through someone else secretly, which read: "All friends are well and happy and are anxiously waiting to welcome you. We see no reason for you to be where you are when there is so much to be done outside."

This message made Bose anxious to get our of jail as soon as possible. Since the detention order was expected to continue until the end of the war, he wrote to the Home Minister and said, in part:

> There is no other alternative for me but to register a moral purpose against the unjust act of this indefinite detention and as the proof of that protest to take a voluntary fast unto death ... Life under existing conditions is intolerable for me ... the government is bent on holding me in jail by brute force ... release me or I shall refuse to live and it is for me to decide whether I choose to live or die ... The individual must die so the nation may live. Today I must die so that India may live, may win freedom and glory.

Subhas Chandra Bose started his hunger strike on November 29, 1940. The Government had to lift the detention order in view of his quickly deteriorating health. But he was kept under house arrest. Police watched his house round the clock. Unfortunately, six months of imprisonment in India and the week-long fast shattered his health to a great extent. After his release on December 5, 1940, he had become physically too emaciated to do any serious work. The restoration of his health while staying at home under house arrest became his urgent need in order to proceed with his risky and very strenuous adventure. So, he remained confined to his room, eating a restorative diet, while growing a beard and mustache to help disguise himself.

He also isolated himself from visitors. Only his "Boudi," wife of his brother Sarat Bose, his two nephews (Aurobindo and Sisir), niece Ila, mother Prabhabati and his two personal physicians (Dr. M.N. Roy and Dr. Pancharan Chatterjee) could meet him.

Subhas Chandra Bose kept the plan and the arrangements of his adventurous escape strictly secret, even from those who were allowed to meet him. He told his brother, Sarat Bose, and nephew, Sisir, about his plans only two days before his exit from the house. Funds for his secret plan were collected by the All India Forward Bloc from all sources and passed on to him. His personal effects, which had the appearance of belonging to a Muslim gentleman, were purchased secretly and hurriedly by Sisir Bose, with the guidance of Mian Akbar Shah. They were packed into a suitcase, an attaché case and a bed roll prominently marked with the initials "M.Z."

That was because he intended to travel disguised as Mohammad Ziauddin, a Jubbulpore-based Moulvi (Muslim doctor of law, or imam). The owner of India Assurance Co. Ltd., Mian Akbar Shah, a member of Forward Bloc from North West Frontier Province, was to escort him all the way from Calcutta to Peshawar.

In Muslim fashion, Bose's clothes were stitched to his size by a tailor conducted secretly to him for taking the measurements. Sisir Bose, well prepared with instructions from his Uncle Subhas, was to drive the car "Wanderer," taking him to Bareree, in Bihar, where Asoke Bose, the eldest son of Sarat Bose, a mining engineer, lived with his wife. After a day's rest there, he was to board the Delhi Kalka Mail train, to change for Peshawar at Delhi.

At 1:30 am on January 17, 1941, when all the members of the family, including the servants, were fast asleep, and even the C.I.D. men on the road outside were snoring under their blankets, Subhas Chandra Bose, disguised as Ziauddin, quietly slipped out of the house. He was driven away by Sisir towards Bareree. Only Ila, Aurobindo and Dwijendra Bose, son of their eldest uncle, were awake to bid goodbye to their Uncle Subhas.

As planned, he reached Bareree the next morning and boarded Kalka Mail the same day after midnight. To give an impression that he was writing letters as usual from seclusion, Subhas Chandra Bose had prepared a number of letters bearing different dates and addressed to different people with instructions for them to be posted gradually according to their dates after his departure.

He had also left a number of slips of paper roughly scribbled in a casual manner explaining his inability to meet anyone, as he was observing complete silence in connection with his meditation. These were to be handed to visitors asking to meet him.

Furthermore, Ila, Sisir (after his immediate return from Bareree), Aurobindo and their eldest uncle's son Dwijendra, who was politically active with Subhas Chandra Bose, were advised to be seen around his room as usual to make a show of attending to his needs. The cook served his meals in "thali," pushing them behind the screen in front of his room, coming back later to removed the emptied thali. But it was actually Ila who consumed the food quietly from behind the screen.

This drama of showing the usual routine of Subhas Chandra Bose in seclusion engaged in "sadhana," or meditation, was designed to bluff the C.I.D. men for nine days, until he was expected to have crossed the Indian border safely.

But on the morning of Sunday, January 26th, the servant was alarmed to find that the "thali" of meals served on Saturday night remained untouched. After he informed Ila about it, a frantic search for Subhas Chandra Bose ensued. Finding him nowhere in the house at Elgin Road, they looked around the Woodburn Park house of Sarat Bose, not far from there. Since a pair of Subhas Chandra Bose's old shoes was found missing from the Elgin Road house, while all his other belongings remained, it was assumed that he must have left at night wearing those old shoes.

When the news of his sudden disappearance was disclosed, it went like wild fire throughout the country and the world. A wild goose chase in search of Subhas Chandra Bose was conducted by family members, friends and the government police department but to no avail. He had gone out of the country in pursuance of his life's mission to liberate India. In order to organize an armed struggle from outside India, he was prepared to seek foreign help from any powerful nation, irrespective of the ideological and political views adopted by them. That is clear from what he said on May 1, 1942, in Germany:

"I am not an apologist of the three powers and it is not my task to defend what they have done or may do in the future. That is a task which devolves on these nations themselves. My concern is, however, with India and, if I may add further, with India alone."

On March 31, 1941, Sisir Bose received a letter addressed to his father, Sarat Bose, written in Bengali by Subhas Chandra Bose from Kabul, along with a message entitled, "A Message to My Countrymen from somewhere in Europe" and a long article entitled, "Forward Bloc: It's Justification." Those had been brought by Bhagat Ram Talwar, who had just returned to India after escorting Subhas Chandra Bose from Peshawar to Kabul, after seeing him off on March 18, 1941, en route to Berlin, via Moscow, by car, train and plane journeys. A page culled from his article on Forward Bloc reads:

(a) The propaganda and activities of the Forward Bloc have been responsible for inducing Congress and Mahatma Gandhi to give the go-by to the original stand of the latter in September, 1939, with reference to the war and to return to the war policy advocated by the Congress from 1927 to 1938.

(b) In building up the Left Movement, the Forward Bloc has clarified the issue which separates the Left from the Right and has stimulated the intellectual and ideological progress of the Congress.

7

(c) The Forward Bloc has been functioning as a watchdog for warning the Congress and the country against any backsliding on the part of any individual or party – particularly with reference to the major issue of the war crisis and national struggle with reference to the future it may be confidentially asserted.

The Forward Bloc, beginning in mid-April, 1939, less than 18 months before Subhas Chandra Bose's mysterious disappearance, had gathered under its banner the largest number of youth constituting the "sinews of the Indian nation." Bose, while informing people of his safety after the disappearance, was in this way highlighting the power of youth in action through his newborn Forward Bloc by delineating its achievements within that short period.

Netaji Subhas Chandra Bose, the Sepah-Salar *(Commander-in-Chief) of the Azad Hind Fauj.*

Netaji Subhas Chandra Bose was the only Indian leader in the twentieth century who could unite Indians living in Southeast

Asia, irrespective of caste, creed, linguistic and religious differences or social status. That is why even Gandhiji, who was the ideological opponent of Subhas Chandra Bose, was ultimately led to say publicly:

> The hypnotism of the Indian National Army led by Netaji has cast its spell upon us. Netaji's name is one to conjure with. His bravery shines through all actions. The great lesson that we can draw from his life is the way in which he infused the spirit of Unity amongst his men and women so that they could rise above all the religious and provincial barriers and shed together their blood for the common cause.

---

1. See https://en.wikipedia.org/wiki/All_India_Forward_Bloc
2. See http://en.banglapedia.org/index.php?title=Bengal_Provincial_Congress
3. Rash Behari Bose was a co-founder of the INA, which he later handed over to Subhas Chandra Bose. See https://en.wikipedia.org/wiki/Rash_Behari_Bose.
4. Siraj ud-Daulah was the last independent ruler of Bengal. The Howell Memorial Monument was set up in Calcutta to commemorate the death of English captives in the Black Hole of Calcutta incident, for which Siraj ud-Daulah was partially responsible. See https://en.wikipedia.org/wiki/Siraj_ud-Daulah

MATCH MADE IN HEAVEN

*E*pical indeed is the wholehearted dedication of a super patriot. For the first and last time in his life, Subhas Chandra Bose caressed and kissed his first-born infant, Anita, and left her in the arms of his brave bride to undertake a perilous war-time journey by sea from Germany to Japan. As he made his way through the hazardous maze of enemy war ships, he knew full well that he might never survive the journey. This is a reminder that even the great men in the world, from any country, are human beings with all the natural human tendencies.

Netaji with wife Emilie Schenkl in Germany.

Our Netaji, the unparalleled Indian leader of the twentieth century, was no exception to nature's law in this regard. One of his love letters to his Austrian lady love, provided below, shows his singular love for Emilie Schenkl[1], the woman who chose to be his wife for the sake of selfless love.

The story that follows the letter will show how much a great patriot sacrificed for the mission of his life to emancipate his motherland from foreign bondage. In this manner, Netaji emulated Lord Gautama Buddha, who in a similar way, left his loving wife and infant son to emancipate humanity's suffering due to ignorance. The letter reads:

My Darling,

Even the iceberg sometimes melt and so it is with me now. I can no longer restrain myself from penning these few lines to convey my deep love for you – my darling – or as we would say in our own way – the queen of my heart. But do you love me – do you care for me – do you long for me? You called me 'pranadhik' (meaning more than life) but did you mean it? Do you love me more than your own life? Is that possible?

With Indian Hindus, it may be possible – for a Hindu woman has, for centuries, given up her life for the sake of her husband, whom she worships like God. But you Europeans have a different tradition. Moreover, why should you love me more than your own life? I am like a wandering bird that comes from afar, remains for a while, and then flies away to its distant home. For such a person, why should you cherish so much love?

My dearest! In a few weeks, I must fly to my distant home. My country calls me, my duty calls me – I must leave you and go back to my 'first love,' my country.

So often I have told you that I have already sold myself to my first love. I have very little left to give to anyone. What little I have – I have given you. It may not be worthy of you and your great love for me – but that is all that I have to give you and you cannot expect anything more from me.

I do not know what the future has in store for me. Maybe, I shall spend my life in prison, maybe I shall be shot or hanged. But whatever happens, I shall think of you and convey my gratitude to you in silence for your love for me. Maybe I shall never see you again – maybe I shall not be able to write to you again when I am back – but believe me, you will always live in my heart, in my thoughts and in my dreams. If fate should thus separate us in this life I shall long for you in my next life. And if you believe in my religion – pray similarly.

My angel! I thank you for loving me and teaching me to love you. My sweetest! Be a good girl – and above all, be unselfish. Care not for any sorrow or suffering that may come. Sorrow and suffering cannot make you unhappy, if you are unselfish. If you are selfish, nothing can make you happy. This is the only advice I can give you – I, your 'guru' (I think you called me as such). I hate selfishness and I dislike selfish people. You have an unselfish heart – that is why I could love you. Make that heart more and more unselfish and you will increase your happiness in this life and after.

My queen! Should we not meet again after I leave Europe, think kindly of me. Do not blame me for not loving you more. I have given what I had – how can I give you more? With these lines, I send you the tears that are now flowing.

I never thought before that a woman's love could ensnare me. So many did love me before, but I never looked at them. But you, naughty woman, have caught me. And why?

Is this love of any earthly use? We who belong to two different lands, have we anything in common? My country, my people, my traditions, my habits and customs, my climate, in fact everything, is so different from yours. Then why do you love me? And what is it that you love? What is there in me that attracts and compels you to love? Can't you tell?

For the moment, I have forgotten all these differences that separate our countries. I have loved the woman in you – the soul in you. You are the first woman I have loved. God grant that you may also be the last.

– Adieu my dearest.

This letter, written in March 1936, just before his return to India, after the three-year exile in Europe, is more than enough to show the selfless love that Netaji had for the only woman he loved in his life.

Now we come to the story of their secret wedding and the subsequent short period of their matrimonial life, about three years and three months, which led to the birth of their daughter Anita.

Netaji's wife Emilie with daughter Anita in Germany.

The intimacy of Subhas Chandra Bose with his young Austrian typist, Fraulein (Miss) Emilie Schenkl, grew when they lived in close association during his exile in Europe during the mid-1930s. Their emotional attachment deepened with regular correspondence after his return to India in April 1936, throughout his imprisonment, house arrest and, later, his stay at the health resort at Dalhousie (now in Himachal Pradesh). During his short visit to Badgastein, the famous health resort in Austria, she stayed with him again to help him write his autobiography, *An Indian Pilgrim*.[2] There, they tied their nuptial knot on December 26, 1937. The ceremony was performed simply by exchanging garlands in secret, without the consent or presence of parents or relatives. This is an ancient Indian wedding ceremony called "Gandharva Vivah."

Subhas Chandra Bose had to do this in order to satisfy the natural urge from both sides to be dedicated to one another, even though they had no prospect of leading a settled matrimonial life under the prevailing circumstances. However, they did cherish a remote hope of settling in a home as husband and wife, should they survive to see a free India.

Subhas Chandra Bose now had to balance his exclusive love for his country with the love of a woman who wanted nothing but the love and self-satisfaction of being the wife of a great man like Subhas. This explains his anxiety to establish her as a self-supporting, honorable woman. He sent Emilie some money that he earned by writing for Indian papers and journals until she obtained permanent employment in the Posts and Telegraphs Department in May 1938.

Their marriage remained a secret even from her mother, who came to know about their relationship in 1941, during the war, when she came to stay with her. The couple's daughter, Anita, was born during this time. The question arises: why a secret marriage, one that was kept hidden throughout the period of their matrimonial life?

The obvious reason is: as the prospective president of the Indian National Congress, the biggest political organization of the country, Subhas Chandra Bose had reached the pinnacle of power and popularity in the Indian political arena. Being optimistic by nature, and almost sure that India would achieve independence by taking advantage of the imminent world war, he had started planning the future of India after her liberation from British bondage. So far, he had kept his personal life in abeyance.

Emilie Schenkl was the only woman to whom he had become emotionally attached to the extent that he had envisaged her to be his life partner. She was a great source of inspiration for him, which he needed all the more in these difficult times.

By then, his previous ideas on sexual relations had obviously changed. In his book *An Indian Pilgrim,* written at Badgastein during those days, he had categorically placed the development of love at the center of human life. He explained that in his youth, he expended a lot of his energy in controlling and suppressing his sexual passions. He wrote in the book, "As I have gradually turned from a purely spiritual ideal to a life of social service, my views of sex have undergone transformation."

By then, he had begun viewing the sexual instinct as a natural phenomenon that need not be suppressed. So, with that change in his point of view, the previously self-imposed ban on marriage was off. However, at that juncture of his life, marriage would have hampered his more weighty national responsibility as the prospective future president of the Indian National Congress. In view of the imminent Second World War, he had definite plans for organizing and launching a country-wide movement, taking advantage of the wartime conditions, to wrest India from British rule.

Subhas Chandra Bose tried to express his emotions in the last couple of letters he wrote to Emilie from Dalhousie before he reached Badgastein towards the end of 1937. The first one, written in block letters, reads:

I have been longing to write to you for some time past – but you can easily understand how difficult it was to write to you about my feelings. I just want to let you know that I am exactly what I was before when you knew me. Not a single day passes that I do not think of you. You are with me all the time. I cannot possibly think of anyone else in this world. I cannot tell you how lonely I have been feeling all these months and how sorrowful. Only one thing could make me happy – but I do not know if that is possible. However, I am thinking of it day and night – praying to God to show me the right path.

Though thinking of Emilie all the time as he wrote to her, he continued his quest for spiritual contemplation and meditation. In a letter written to a friend on August 8, 1937, only about four and a half months before his nuptial ties with Emilie, he said, "I believe in God and also in prayer. The mental and spiritual exercise that I have been doing is of two kinds … practice of self-assertion. The other is self-surrender … and try to merge my existence in it (i.e. a mighty stream of Divine energy which flows through me. I never pray for anything material. It is mean and sordid.)"

In this connection, it is worth recalling the last portion of a letter to Emilie that he wrote in March 1936: "Just one thing more before I close this long letter. For your life, never pray for any selfish object or aim. Always pray for what is good for humanity… for what is good in the eyes of God – what is good for all time. Pray in a "nishkarna" (i.e. without expectation of gain)."

Within a month after reaching Dalhousie for rest and recuperation, he wrote to her on June 17, 1937:

My advice to you for the future would be as follows:

(1) To keep your body fit, do exercise regularly. In Vienna, you can join a gymnastic school, like the one I used to join.

(2) To make yourself useful in later life, take lessons in

domestic hygiene, domestic economy, household management etc.

(3) Also take training to be a competent secretary. For this, it is necessary to know book-keeping, a bit of accountancy and how to handle and arrange files.

(4) Learn some music … including playing some instrument … so that you can entertain yourself and also your family at times.

(5) Learn as many languages as possible. It is more necessary to speak.

(6) You should know something of needlework, knitting, embroidery, etc.

(7) Regarding the subjects you should study, you may choose a subject which will fit in with your future work. Over and above this, you should study a little philosophy.

In a subsequent letter written to her in German, on June 24, he further says: "When you have time, please read the *Bhagwat Gita* and also Garner's book in English on the *Art of Governance*. This will greatly help your intellectual development."

In another letter, written on August 5, 1937, he chided her: "It is not good that you smoke cigarettes … It is better you prepare everything for your future life. One must always work." Further, on September 16, in a letter written in German, he categorically asks her, "If you have enough time in Vienna and if it is possible and if you find a teacher, then please do learn our language." He also urged her to learn spinning, which she started on her own.

Netaji with Emilie and friends in Germany.

Towards the end of 1937, he grew more and more emotional towards Emilie. He had started writing in German, advising her also to do the same, probably to maintain secrecy. These earnest instructions given to a young lady who was only his typist in the past indicate that he had started envisaging her to be his life partner in the future. With all his devotion and dedication to the emancipation of his motherland, he was also a normal human being and had all the natural tendencies that one should have.

So, there was nothing wrong in his marrying Emilie, whom he had started loving in the normal course of close contact. She knew very well that, as the wife of a great patriot like Subhas Chandra Bose, who was always ready to risk his life for the sake of his country, she could not expect a settled matrimonial life.

Yet, she agreed to marry him, in the face of expected life-long separation. Both of them were prepared to live in one another's memories. There was no hindrance to Emilie re-marrying a suitable Austrian to share the burden of her life, but she said there was "no vacancy in her heart" for anyone else. Netaji remained the sole occupant of her heart, even after having disappeared forever.

From July 6, 1939, until April 3, 1941, no communication was possible between the two, even through correspondence. The obvious reason is that Netaji was too seriously involved in politics during the Second World War, as he had to be clandestinely busy with his plans to escape from India to open a "second front" for the war of Indian Independence. Then, suddenly, like a bolt from the blue, Emilie had the pleasant surprise of getting a telegram on April 3, 1941, from the German Foreign Office informing her: "Bose is now in Berlin and asks you, if possible, to come here immediately. Confirm."

Subsequently she received his letter of the same date written from Berlin. As their secret marriage was then unknown, even to Emilie's mother and sister, Subhas Chandra Bose had to address her as "Fraulein (Miss) Emilie Schenkl" in a normal way and request her to join him in Berlin, with language couched as if seeking secretarial assistance. He had written, "It is possible that I may need a secretary here. If so, can you come? Will your mother and sister agree to it?"

In addition to keeping their marriage a secret, she was required to maintain another subterfuge by recognizing and addressing him as Signor Orlando Mazzotta. He advised her, in the strictly confidential letter, that in order to encourage her mother and sister to send her to work with him in Berlin, she should tell them that he was traveling under the name Orlando Mazzotta and request them to keep the secret. Emilie at once sought sabbatical leave from her permanent postal job and rushed to Berlin to meet Subhas Chandra Bose, now posing as Signor Mazzotta.

His arrival in Berlin with an Italian diplomatic passport provided her a chance to stay with him as his wife, though ironically as his supposed secretary cum personal assistant. So, Subhas. in the guise of an Italian, met his "virgin wife," whom he had married clandestinely at Badgastein about three years and three months before and then had to leave her without enjoying even a honeymoon, due to his unavoidable political work in India.

The irony of his unsettled life led him to have his "Suhag Raat" with his bride Emilie, not as the Indian patriot Subhas Chandra Bose, but as an Italian in Germany far away from his home in India.

Subhas Chandra Bose, posing as an Italian for about a year, had to adapt himself to the European style of life and start smoking cigarettes, drink alcohol moderately and dress in European fashion. Emilie lived with him as his wife in the guise of his secretary throughout the period of his stay in Europe between April 1941 and February 8, 1943.

Except for three months, when Emilie went back to her mother in Vienna for the delivery of their daughter, Anita, born on November 29, 1941, the couple stayed in posh Berlin hotels, eventually moving into a grand house at Sophianstrasse in Charlotteuberg, where Emilie enjoyed the same high standard of living as that provided to Subhas by the German government's Foreign Office.

That period of their matrimonial life, about one and a half years, ended forever with the departure of Netaji on his journey to Southeast Asia to lead the Indian National Army (INA) as its Supreme Commander.

Netaji with the three main high ranking officers of the Azad Hind Fauj: Col. Dhillon, Col. Sahgal and Col. Shah Nawaz.

After Netaji left, Emilie played an important role in keeping the secrecy of his departure by remaining in the Sophianstrasse villa while Anita stayed with her mother in Vienna. Pretending to be living with Netaji, she would tell people who enquired on the phone that he had gone on a short trip for some urgent business, or that he was simply too busy to meet anyone. She posted his predated letters written before the departure on the relevant dates, and saw that his recorded speeches were broadcast later to suggest that he was still present in Berlin.

At times, she would even bluff the cook, asking him not to prepare Bose's food, as he was out of the house for a few days. Sometimes, she would pretend to serve his meals in his room, since he was supposedly too busy to eat in the dining room.

After putting on this show for some time, she relinquished the villa to the German Foreign Office, which allotted it to Netaji's colleague A.C.N. Nambiar, who continued to work at the Free India Centre.[3] Then, she left for Vienna to resume her job at the postal service and to raise her infant daughter. Netaji lived in her memories for the rest of her life, which ended in March 1996.

Netaji was conscientious enough as a husband to try to make sure that his wife and daughter were duly recognized and given respect by his family members in India in the event of his not surviving the perilous wartime submarine journey to Japan or, later, the hazards of the war. So he wrote a letter in Bengali to his elder brother, Sarat Chandra Bose, in India, asking him to give the same love and care to his wife and daughter as he had received himself.

The English translation of the letter is as follows:

"My respected brother,
      Today, once again, I am embarking on the path of danger. But this time, towards home. I may not see the end of this road. If I meet with any such danger, I will not be able to send you any

news in this life. That is why I am leaving the news here; it will reach you in due time. I have married here and have a daughter. In my absence, please show my wife and daughter the love that you have given me throughout your life. May my wife and daughter complete and successfully fulfill my unfinished tasks – that is my ultimate prayer.

Please accept my salutations and convey the same to
Mother, Mejobowdidi and other elders.
Berlin, February 8, 1943.

Your devoted brother,
Subhas"

Although he had expressed his hope that his wife and daughter would one day complete successfully his unfinished tasks, Emilie Schenkl Bose had her own limitations. Her first and foremost responsibility was to bring up and provide the best possible education to their daughter Anita, in the face of the war-shattered condition of her own country. And unfortunately, the letter Netaji sent to Sarat Bose did not reach him until after the war. So, she faced the hardships of life during the war with her infant daughter and old mother to look after.

She struggled on, maintaining her self-respect as the wife of a great Indian patriot – Netaji Subhas Chandra Bose. She did bring up and educate her daughter successfully. But because of the circumstances under which she had to live, she could not be expected to complete the unfinished task left by her husband to be carried on in India, though she would very much have liked to do so had circumstances permitted.

Later, in 1948, Sarat Bose finally received the letter sent to him by Subhas Chandra Bose. He traveled to Europe with his wife, two daughters and son, Sisir Bose, to meet Emilie Bose and her daughter Anita, to accept them into his family. By then, Anita was six years old and had already started going to school. Emilie was also, by then, well settled, after the war time and post-war hardships. It was not possible for Emilie Bose to return to India with the Bose family and leave her old and dependent mother helpless in Vienna. So, Anita had no chance to be brought up and educated in India to be able to fulfill the aspirations of her great father, Netaji Subhas Chandra Bose.[4]

Anita Bose, while studying in America for her post-graduate degree, came in contact with Martin Pfaff, a fellow student who had previously studied in India between 1958 and 1962 for his B-Com degree and Social Work Education for the Blind. With him being a German national and lover of India, they drew nearer to one another and ultimately married and settled in Germany, living in Stadtberfenin Augsburg, where they both taught as professors of Economics at the University of Augsburg. They have two sons, Peter Arun and Thomas Krishna, and a daughter, Maya.

I had the opportunity of meeting Dr. Anita Bose Pfaff during one of her visits to India with her husband. I feel strongly that if this only and talented child of Netaji could have had the opportunity of being brought up and educated in India, and been domiciled here, that she would definitely have been able to fulfill the last hopes and aspirations of her great father Netaji. She would have proven herself in no less a way than did Indira Gandhi, the only child of Jawaharlal Nehru, the one-time close friend and colleague and, later, great political rival of her father.

Emilie Schenkl Bose, despite her keen desire to travel to India with Netaji, remained in Vienna. She could never be persuaded to come to India without Netaji.

The writer of this book expresses her deep sense of reverence to the memory of Shrimati Emilie Schenkl Bose, the better half of her immortal husband Netaji Subhas Chandra Bose, for her enormous fortitude and courage, her self-respect and independent nature, her love for India and, above all, her selfless devotion to

Netaji, which rivaled that of any Indian woman who is revered as "pativrata sati."

---

1. For more on Emilie Schenkl, see https://en.wikipedia.org/wiki/Emilie_Schenkl
2. The book is available in the U.S. on Amazon.
3. Nambiar was an interesting character in his own right, with close connections to the Soviet Union. See https://en.wikipedia.org/wiki/A._C._N._Nambiar. For more on the Free India Centre, see https://en.wikipedia.org/wiki/Free_India_Centre
4. For more on Anita Bose Pfaff, see https://en.wikipedia.org/wiki/Anita_Bose_Pfaff

THE EMERGENCE OF THE RANI
JHANSI REGIMENT

&

*B*elieving in the idea of women's liberation, Netaji's decision to add a women's regiment to his Indian National Army first took root in 1928, when he organized the Congress Volunteer Corps in Calcutta.[1]

Capt. Latika Ghosh in the Congress was in charge of the Volunteer Corps and did excellent work to raise the status of women and bring them to the same level as the men, giving them equal opportunities for active participation in social and political fields.[2]

While voyaging in the submarine on a 93-day perilous journey from Germany to the Far East, Subhas Chandra Bose revived his old dream of an armed unit of women as he planned his future work in Asia.[3] Netaji wanted to name unit the "Rani Jhansi Regiment" after the brave Rani Laxmibai of Jhansi.[4] While narrating the story of her bravery fighting against the British forces in the First War of Independence in 1857 to his assistant Abid Hasan, he quoted remarks by General Hugh Rose, who had faced the Rani at the battlefield near Kalpi:

"If there had been one thousand Indian women as brave as the Rani of Jhansi, we would have never conquered India."

Netaji's inherent faith in "Nari Shakti" (Women's Empower-
ment) and the bravery of women in Indian history made him
determined to raise a women's regiment. For him, the idea served
a double purpose – one, to make the womenfolk free, and the
other to enable them to gain self-confidence from their training
to help them in their future lives.

The historian Geraldine Forbes expressed her appreciation of
the contribution of Subhas Chandra Bose in the social and political boosting of women by saying, "If there was a living figure
who encouraged the activities of women, it was Subhas Chandra
Bose, who is considered by many of the women revolutionaries as
Bengal's greatest champion of 'women rights.'"

He considered their participation in the freedom struggles to
be essential. There had not been, in the history of the world, a
single instance of a fully trained and armed women's fighting
force as large as this Rani Jhansi Regiment, though there have
been some rare cases of soldier-like, brave women fighting for a
just cause or for their rights, singularly or in small groups. The
Rani Jhansi Regiment, as envisaged and organized by Netaji in his
INA, was the first of its kind in the whole world.[5]

After reaching Southeast Asia from Germany, Netaji took
charge of the civil and military organizations, namely, the Indian
Independence League and the Indian National Army, that were
already set up by Rash Behari Bose, his predecessor, who retired
due to ill health. After reorganizing and revitalizing them in a few
days, he spoke to Dr. Lakshmi Sehgal nee Swaminathan, who was
the first bold and promising young Indian lady to have met him,
about the urgency of active participation of women in this movement.[6] She responded to him immediately and worked intensely
to organize a women's meeting to be addressed by Netaji on July
12, 1943.

Netaji and Capt. Lakshmi Swaminathan inspecting the Ranis during Guard of Honor and bayonet practice.

To give him a pleasant surprise, she arranged for a squad of 20 women to be trained and armed in a short period of time to receive him as a Women's Guard of Honor.[7] Amidst thunderous ovations and shouted slogans of "Netaji Zindabad (Long Live the Revered Leader)," "Azad Hind Zinadabad (Long Live Free Hindustan)" and "Chalo Delhi (On to Delhi)," he spoke to them concerning the condition of their enslaved motherland. He referred to Rani Laxmibai of Jhansi, her valor and bravery, and how he had formed a regiment and named it after her.

He further spoke of his desire to have 1,000 fully trained and equipped Ranis in the Women's Regiment of the INA to be sure of success in this last and decisive war of Indian Independence. He requested the female audience to give their names and enroll themselves in the great cause.

This most impressive speech, followed by Netaji's forceful appeal, brought about the birth of his brainchild, the Rani Jhansi Regiment. Training started soon after the enrollment procedure was over. The Ranis, who came from Thailand, Malaysia, Singapore and Burma, all loved their country – India – so much that they were prepared to sacrifice and work for its freedom.

Netaji personally selected non-commissioned officers from among INA veterans to train the Ranis. The charismatic appeal of Netaji brought about a lot of enthusiasm. As a result, more than 1,000 Ranis enlisted for the military training. At first, the training started in temporary camps, until permanent camps were established. The Ranis were given the same training as that of male soldiers using rifles, revolvers, hand-grenades, Bren guns (machine guns) and bayonets.

Capt. Lakshmi Swaminathan saluting Netaji as the Rani of Jhansi Regiment reports in battle formation.

Their daily routine started at 6 a.m. with flag-hoisting, followed by brisk physical exercises in squads, referred to as "P.T." (Physical Training). After breakfast, classes on various subjects were held in three-hour periods. Following lunch and a short rest, the training continued with parades, drills, use of arms, bayonet practice, etc. until the evening. The day ended with unfurling the flag known as "Jhanda Salami," followed by singing of the National Anthem.

The literate and educated recruits could advance faster and had the opportunity to be promoted to the ranks of non-commissioned and commissioned officers, according to their abilities and achievements. This is where my story starts, entwined with India's freedom struggle and inspired by the brave son of India, Netaji Subhas Chandra Bose.

Ranis training immediately after joining the regiment. Uniforms were given later.

Ranis under training with their rifles and uniforms.

I took up the training very seriously and progressed extremely well, both in the military training as well as in the nurses section. Capt. Lakshmi was very proud of me and happy about my achievements. She always recommended me for higher promotion, which helped me to become an officer.

---

1. For photo of Bose in Congress Volunteer Corps uniform, see https://commons.wikimedia.org/wiki/File:Subhas_C._Bose_001.jpg
2. For more on Latika Ghosh and her work, see https://en.wikipedia.org/wiki/Mahila_Rashtriya_Sangha
3. For a fascinating account of this submarine journey, see https://www.thebetterindia.com/83132/subhash-chandra-bose-india-submarine-germany-japan/
4. For more on the story of Rani Laxmibai of Jhansi, see https://en.wikipedia.org/wiki/Rani_of_Jhansi.
5. For the best in-depth account of the Rani Jhansi regiment, see *Women at War: Subhas Chandra Bose and the Rani of Jhansi Regiment* by Vera Hildebrand

(Harper Collins, 2016). Between 2008 and 2011, Hildebrand interviewed all the surviving Ranis she could find, 22 in all, including Rama Khandwala, who is mentioned frequently in the book. Hildebrand also gained access to interrogation reports that British intelligence officers conducted with Ranis after the war. Also see https://en.wikipedia.org/wiki/Rani_of_Jhansi_Regiment.

6. For more on this pivotal figure in the history of the Rani Jhansi Regiment, see https://en.wikipedia.org/wiki/Lakshmi_Sahgal. For Sehgal's own story of her role in the regiment, see https://www.ndtv.com/india-news/my-days-in-the-indian-national-army-by-lakshmi-sahgal-493887. Hildebrand mentions frequently in her book how Sehgal's account does not always match up with the recollection of other Ranis.

7. For more details on how the honor guard was organized by Lakshmi Sahgal and later developed into the Rani of Jhansi Regiment, see https://ink.library.smu.edu.sg/cgi/viewcontent.cgi?article=2644&context=soss_research

NETAJI WITH THE BRAVE RANIS AT MAYMYO

⚜

*L*ilavati Chhaganlal Mehta, my beloved mother, a very dominating, spiritual personality, beautifully attired with exquisite taste in jewelry, was in tune with her father-in-law Dr. Pranjiwan Jagjivan Mehta's thoughts about working aggressively for India's freedom. She was selected as a volunteer to work for the Indian Independence League in Rangoon in 1943.[1] Her job was to collect funds for the Azad Hind Fauj, or INA.

Rama (right) with sister Neelam (left) and mother Lilavati Chhanganlal Mehta (center).

My mother was then selected as the recruiting officer for the Rani Jhansi Regiment.[2] Her first two recruits were myself and my sister, Neelam Chhaganlal Mehta.[3] We joined as ordinary "sepoys" (privates) and were given military training.[4] According to each one's capabilities, we got promoted to the rank of "havaldar" (sergeant), then "sub-officer" and later second lieutenant.

Rama (right) with sister Neelam.

I had a loud voice and could bellow, "Aage badho (March ahead)!" I was made the platoon commander with 30 Ranis behind me. Due to my hard work, and because I took my training in military warfare as well as the nurses section very seriously, I had the backing of Captain Laxmi Sehgal, who kept on promoting me. She was very proud of my achievements.

Netaji was extremely protective and concerned about the Ranis (the "Queens") and hence would not permit us to go to the frontline.[5] But some of us were very eager to go to the front, where there was lot of action and work. Then we learned that Col. A.C. Chatterjee was to take charge as governor of the liberated areas in India, after they were freed from British rule. He had been ordered by Netaji to join the Japanese advance on Imphal, in northwestern India.[6]

We took the opportunity to meet Col. Chatterjee personally and expressed our desire to accompany him and to help him start another Rani Jhansi Regiment camp at Maymyo, in northern Burma.[7] Fortunately, Col. A.C. Chatterjee agreed and ordered us to be ready to travel the following day.

Rama joined the Rani Jhansi Regiment of the Azad Hind Fauj on October 21, 1943.

My friend, Havaldar Shakuntala Gandhi, was given charge of the contingent of Ranis. Lt. Manwati Arya came with us as well, although in the capacity as a civilian officer. She served as secretary in the women's department of the Provisional Government of Azad Hind, which had been formed by Netaji Subhas Chandra Bose.[8]

Rama with rifle.

The journey from Rangoon to Maymyo took five days. Before leaving, we took our baggage to headquarters, where a truck was waiting to take us to Maymyo. Military kits were issued to us then. At first there were only 12 of us Ranis. Later on, more Ranis joined us at the Maymyo camp.

As we drove from the Rangoon headquarters in the truck, the Ranis shouted slogans of "Chalo Delhi (On to Delhi)," "Netaji Zindabad (Long live the Revered Leader)," and "Azad Hind Zindabad (Long live free Hindustan)." The Ranis became particularly happy to find their truck traveling behind Netaji's car, which was accompanied by a number of vehicles carrying his entourage of officers, staff and bodyguards.

Rama at target practice immediately after joining the Rani Jhansi Regiment.

Late in the evening, we reached Zayawadi, where we stopped for the day to have our meals. We parked in a big orchard plantation full of dense trees sheltering all the vehicles from the view of enemy planes. Netaji's car was parked near our truck. He came out to talk to us and make inquiries about the Ranis and how they were coping. He was happy to find that all of us were in great spirits and in good health.

During this break, we received the same food in our mess tins that was served to everyone in the INA group. Netaji treated the Ranis the same as all INA soldiers and officers. We had to follow the same discipline, rules and regulations as everyone else. After the meal, we had time to rest and sleep, stretching out in whatever convenient place we could find in the orchard. It was very quiet and peaceful. In the early morning, we could hear the birds twittering.

We continued with our journey and reached our destination. Maymyo is a hill station that the British government had used as Burma's summer capital. Netaji set up his advance headquarters there, as well as the advance camp of the Rani Jhansi Regiment. A Japanese military headquarters and an INA base hospital were already established there.

We were temporarily accommodated in a spacious school building, which included a big bungalow that had been the principal's residence. Netaji and his officers occupied the principal's bungalow and set up their offices there.

All the Ranis started working in the hospital, we had to put in long hours attending to soldiers suffering from wounds or from malaria and other viral diseases. We could hardly get time to eat our meals. It was a heart-wrenching sight as dying soldiers would give us messages to pass on to their loved ones. Looking after soldiers who had lost their limbs was not for the faint hearted.

Havaldar Shakuntala Gandhi (later Shakuntala Shah) and I became very good friends and shared all our emotions about work-related issues, anxieties, moments of happiness, experiences, day to day problems and difficulties. We supported each other and tried to be helpful in whatever way we could.

Later on, after the war was over, she got married and settled in Bombay, like me, and we continued to meet each other to exchange our views on the new challenges that we faced in our lives. I was very sad when she passed away in 2007.

At the time our group had left Rangoon for Maymyo, Capt. Lakshmi Seghal nee Swaminathan had gone to Singapore to attend the passing-out parade of the Rani Jhansi Regiment Officers Training Corps on March 31, 1944. On her return to Rangoon, she also journeyed up to Maymyo with 10 Ranis (eight soldiers and two officers) on April 19, 1944.

Although Imphal did not fall to the Japanese army, we received encouraging reports from the front line about the INA's progress and bravery. We were still camping in the school building and occasionally Netaji would visit us to review our activities. He would personally talk to each of us to learn about our work and health and discover if we had any complaints.

Following Capt. Lakshmi's arrival in Maymyo, Netaji told us to arrange and stage an entertainment program, to be followed by dinner for all ranks, which would be served by the officers and

Netaji himself. The Ranis were very talented and arranged a very interesting show. The date fixed was April 30, 1944.

Just a day before the program was scheduled and preparations were going on for the dress-rehearsal, Netaji suddenly issued instructions to perform the show on that very evening, April 29, leaving April 30 to be a rest holiday.

As we were getting ready to stage the entertainment program that evening, the air-raid siren started wailing at full pitch to warn us of approaching enemy planes. We ran from our dormitories to take shelter in the trench that accommodated all the Ranis. Every time we took shelter in the trench, we would take roll-call to check if everyone was in the trench. This time, we found that one of our Ranis named Lily was absent. Lt. Manwati Arya rushed to fetch her, as Lily was sleeping in the sick room with a high temperature. She brought Lily to the trench in the midst of heavy bombing from the enemy planes. The relieved Ranis inside the trench started shouting, "Rani Jhansi Zindabad (Long live the Rani Jhansi)."

Suddenly, the bomber planes came back, in our direction and dropped their bomb just above our shelter and the camp. A deafening sound of explosions followed, from direct hits on our portion of the school building. We put our heads down on our knees, closing our our eyes, ears and mouth tightly with our palms, expecting to be buried en masse then and there.

Within a few minutes, as suddenly as it started, the bombing and the humming sounds stopped, the planes disappeared and we raised our heads to discover that we were alive. After remaining in the shelter a few more minutes and recovering from the shock, we came out into the dusty, dim moonlight to find that our portion of the building had vanished, leaving nothing but a large and deep crater in the ground. It being a wooden building, there was not much debris of brick and mortar. We had lost everything except our lives, with no physical injuries at all.[9]

Fortunately, nothing had happened to the bungalow occupied

by Netaji and the officers living with him, though it was not very far from our place. Immediately, Netaji came with a group of officers, calm and composed, and inquired about our survival from the devastating bombardments. He sent us with some officers to other vacant rooms of the buildings in the complex.[10] These rooms were cleaned immediately and groundsheets spread on the floor for us to spend the rest of the night, until other arrangements could be made. None of us could sleep, as we kept on talking about our near-death experience.

That night I cried a lot. I wanted to go back to my family, whom I missed so much. I wanted my mother to caress me, wanted her love and pampering, wanted to tell her about how I had escaped death. I kept on saying to myself:

There should be no war. There should be no suffering. There should be no destruction. There should be no sorrow. There should be no hatred.

However, there was one silver lining in the black cloud: God was kind and merciful and we all remained alive to continue our life's journeys and to see the Independence of our country. I was surprised to see the calmness, faith and hope on Netaji's face as he conducted his work so confidently, even under such adverse circumstances. He radiated love for his country.

There were two things which helped us to continue the struggle of Independence. One, our vision that our country would be freed from the alien rulers and two, our faith in our leader Netaji Subhas Chandra Bose, who was so dynamic, courageous and bold. He inspired all of us, gave us a lot of strength and prepared us to bravely face all the difficulties, adversities and hardships.

Today after so many years, we owe a lot to Netaji Subhas Chandra Bose for his advice, training, the "do-or-die" spirit, and the love and pride for our country, as he always told us, "Aage bhado (move ahead)." Netaji, you were very great then and even greater now. I sincerely wish there were more Netajis, as the country needs leaders like you.

Netaji Zindabad!

---

1. For more on the Indian Independence League, see https://en.wikipedia.org/wiki/Indian_Independence_League
2. Hildebrand notes that Rama's mother, "a formidable lady," brandished a sword borrowed from an INA officer at these recruiting meetings to inspire enthusiasm. (p. 154-55) Bina Cline, Rama's daughter, recalls that formidable nature well. After losing her voice box to cancer surgery, her grandmother continued to take buses around Mumbai by writing on a small chalkboard she carried with her.
3. By enlisting on the opening day of the training camp in Rangoon, Rama and Neelam — who "had no choice but to join" — became the first two Ranis born in Burma, according to Hildebrand. (p. 154-55)
4. Rama and Neelam were among those fortunate Ranis whose families were wealthy enough to provide them with tailor-made uniforms. All the rest, according to Hildebrand, got outfitted in cotton khaki by camp tailors. (p. 135)
5. This is a controversial subject. Most of the INA records were destroyed at the end of the war. It's not clear whether Bose ever intended for the Ranis to participate in combat or formed the regiment for propaganda purposes. Hilderbrand explores this topic extensively in her book. Whatever Bose's intentions, none of the Ranis ever participated in combat and the closest they got to the fighting was Maymyo, which was hundreds of miles behind the front. They were, however, subject to air raids at various times. All of the Ranis whom Hildebrand interviewed agreed that Bose, who kept the regiment under his personal control, showed great solicitude for their well-being.
6. Imphal was the pivotal battle of the Burma-India campaigns. For more detail see https://en.wikipedia.org/wiki/Battle_of_Imphal
7. Maymyo, now Pyin Oo Lwin, is a hill town near Mandalay and served as the INA's forward headquarters for the campaign against Imphal. See https://en.wikipedia.org/wiki/Battles_and_operations_of_the_Indian_National_Army
8. For more about the provisional government, see https://en.wikipedia.org/wiki/Azad_Hind
9. This bombing attack is described in an interview with Lakshmi Krishnan, who remembers "Rama Mehta" as one of her six closest friends in the Rani Jhansi Regiment. See https://www.thehindu.com/society/history-and-culture/women-in-command-remembering-the-rani-of-jhansi-regiment/article30999665.ece
10. This visit by Netaji after the bombing attack is described in the unpublished memoirs of Lieutenant Colonel Dr. Benoy Kumar Nandy. See https://www.

telegraphindia.com/culture/heritage/old-soldiers-never-die-the-diary-of-an-
unsung-ina-trooper/cid/1682205

ALAS! WAR IS OVER

*D*espite the high hopes of Netaji for India's liberation, the Japanese Army's advance on Imphal in April 1944 failed. Suffering heavily from starvation, disease and exhaustion, the Japanese and our own INA began retreating in early June back to central Burma.

As the Japanese war effort continued to deteriorate, the Rani of Jhansi Regiment was disbanded and its members sent home.[1] I returned to my family in Rangoon. Netaji himself escorted the Malyan contingent of the Ranis to Thailand and then to Malaysia.[2]

The war in Burma continued until May 3, 1945, when Azad Hind Fauj (INA), as well as the Japanese Army, surrendered Rangoon to the British. There were praises for the way our Fauj maintained order in Rangoon before the surrender. There had not been a single case of theft or robbery during the period we had been in charge. The Irrawaddy river was heavily mined by the Japanese and Rangoon could easily have become involved in house-to-house fighting. But the decision was taken to surrender peacefully. Our cause was lost for the moment. We would not waste Indian lives and property for Japanese prestige.

Reports from our Indian Independence League branches showed that our members prevented any harm befalling Indian and Burmese lives and property — a very disciplined force, indeed. Shri Bahaduri who was in charge of the Indian Independence League in Rangoon, was arrested and sent to the Rangoon Jail. Rumor had it that no less than two hundred of our men were sentenced – without any trial — to varying terms of imprisonment.

As soon as disarmament was complete, all INA soldiers were herded to a separate section of the Rangoon Central Jail. Under the supervision of British Indian troops, they were made to undertake road repair, cleaning and sweeping. They were treated as prisoners and had to remain in custody until they were lucky enough to be released.

Those who came home after spending time in the jail had their movements under strict surveillance. Others had to provide large sums of security money to account for their good behavior. Some had to report regularly to the police.

We of the Rani Jhansi Regiment did not escape the attention of the British. They questioned us about our activities and the role of the regiment in the war. I told them boldly that the Rani Jhansi Regiment was part of the Azad Hind Fauj, under the leadership of Netaji Subhas Chandra Bose, and that we had been trained as military soldiers.

Somehow, they did not press me. I wonder if my determined attitude put them off because I was allowed to go home. But I also found that a man began to shadow me as I came home. I did not worry.

In May 1945, my sister and I were put under house arrest for six months. We were not allowed to leave our house at all during that period.[3]

Many of the top ranking officers of the Fauj were put in jail and had to undergo harsh punishment, atrocities and humiliation. Some of them, along with Col. Shahnawaz, Col. Dhillon, and Col.

Sehgal, were taken to the Red Fort for trial. [4] It was only after India got its independence on August 15, 1947, that all the Fauj members were released and given appropriate honor.

As for Netaji Subhas Chanda Bose, he was reported to have died in a plane crash in Taiwan ion August 18, 1945. But many still believe those reports are untrue (see Appendix One). Just before his death, on August 16, he issued a statement to the Indians of East Asia that said:

> I regret more than you do, that your suffering and sacrifice have not born immediate fruit. But they have not gone in vain, because they have ensured the emancipation of our Motherland and will send as an undying inspiration to Indians all over the world. Posterity will bless your name and will talk with pride about your offerings at the alter of India's freedom ...

---

1. For the Ranis from Burma, the disbanding occurred at the Ranis' camp in Rangoon on April 22, 1945, according to Hildebrand. Immediately after breakfast, the women were summoned to the parade ground with their packs and saw three "tongas," or horse-drawn carriages, waiting at the gate. Their commander said, "Just now, you are provided with transports to go home. *Tongas* will take you home, *Jai Hind.*" Rama's mother, who had been notified of the event, brought the family car to the camp to pick up Rama and her sister, Neelam. (p. 181)
2. About 60% of Rani of Jhansi regiment recruits were uneducated girls, typically of Tamil origin, who had worked on the tea estates in Malaysia. See https://openthemagazine.com/lounge/books/rani-of-jhansi-regiment-sisters-in-arms/
3. As Hildebrand puts it, Rama "was directed to stay at her parents' house in Rangoon for six months after leaving camp, but was allowed to continue her studies. A few polite police officers came to the Mehta residence to ask her why she had joined the RJR. She answered that she had enlisted in order to fight for Indian independence. Since she had no answers other than the obvious ones, the interviews were terminated and the police officers left her alone." (p. 220)
4. For more on the Red Fort trials, see https://en.wikipedia.org/wiki/Indian_National_Army_trials

RETURN TO INDIA AND INDIA'S
INDEPENDENCE

$\mathcal{M}$y family and I left Rangoon by ship and returned to India at the end of December 1946. The Jain Yuvak Mandal had arranged for us to tour many parts of India and give lectures about our extremely dynamic leader Netaji Subhas Chandra Bose, Azad Hind Fauj and the struggle for our freedom. My mother's parents – Shri Ratilal M. Sheth and Smt. Vijayaben R. Sheth — lived in Mumbai and so we stayed with them.

I was extremely lucky to witness the Independence of our country and listen to the first speech given on the night of August 15, 1947, by Shri Jawaharlal Nehru. My joy that India received its Independence cannot be described. All throughout the speech, tears were rolling down my face as I was reminded about our great leader Netaji Subhas Chandra Bose, the Azad Hind Fauj, our training as the Ranis and the great struggle for our freedom. I was also sad that the country was split with the emergence of Pakistan.

Remembering the past and going back 74 years ago, when I was in the Rani Jhansi Regiment, I now feel that was the happiest and most memorable period of my life. At first it was hard and tough undergoing the physical training, marching, giving up all the luxury and comforts, such as good food, the love and care of my parents etc. I used to cry a lot.

But after two months, everything changed. After making friends and learning so much about our country, I felt the flame of a deep desire to fight for independence. I felt very proud and honored to be part of the Azad Hind Fauj, whose spirit of "do or die" was unmeasurable.

After India became a Republic on January 26, 1950, I was invited to meet Shri Sardar Vallabhbhai Patel in Mumbai. [1] We discussed many issues and he was very keen to know about Netaji Subhas Chandra Bose, the Rani Jhansi Regiment and Azad Hind Fauj. He requested that I join the Indian National Congress party but I declined. I was not interested in politics, even though I was extremely proud of my country and had a desire to represent my country in some way.

---

1. For more about Vallabhbhai Patel, see https://en.wikipedia.org/wiki/Vallabhbhai_Patel

WHAT GAVE INDIA FREEDOM?

he effects of World War II and the and the tremor of revolt in India's armed forces greatly inspired the English to leave.

According to Clement Attlee, who was Britain's Prime Minister at the time of Independence, the role of the Quit India Movement was minimal.[1]

P.V. Chakraborthy, former chief justice of Calcutta High Court, says in a letter that when he met Attlee in 1956, he had asked the former prime minister: "The Quit India Movement of Gandhi practically died out long before 1947 and there was nothing in the Indian situation at that time which made it necessary for the British to leave in a hurry. Why then did they do so?"

Attlee replied that the Royal Indian Navy Mutiny in 1946 and the activities of the Indian National Army were the main factors.[2]

The role of international politics in India's freedom is beyond dispute. In the first half of the 20th Century, all over the world, the time was up for the British. Without the revolutions of Gandhi, Sri Lanka won its freedom in 1948. It was not a coincidence that Sri Lanka's meeting with destiny occurred around the same time as it did in India. The world was changing, and it was in Britain's interest to step back.

---

1. For more on the Quit India movement, see https://en.wikipedia.org/wiki/Quit_India_Movement
2. The naval mutiny, which began in Mumbai, ultimately involved 20,000 sailors. See https://en.wikipedia.org/wiki/Royal_Indian_Navy_mutiny

AND LIFE GOES ON ...

*S*ince I knew shorthand and typing, I started to work as
secretary and personal assistant in a trading firm. I gave
up the job after marrying Satyendra Mangaldas Khandwala in
December 1949. At that time, I had this queer notion that my
father-in-law would not want me to work and would want me to
be a housewife.

Rama with her husband, Satyendra Mangaldas Khandwala.

After idling for six months, I became bored and unhappy

wasting such precious time. So, one day, I boldly asked my father-in-law if I could start working again. To my surprise, he agreed and I was very lucky to get a job as a secretary near my home at Opera House in a firm called "Hindco."[1] Before getting the job, I had to prove my English language skills by writing an essay and submit the same to the director of the company, Mr. D.M. Desai.

One day, when I was working in the office, I came across an advertisement from the Government of India Tourist office in Mumbai announcing that they were offering a tourist guide training course for three months and that preference would be given to persons who had foreign language skills. I had learned the Japanese language in Rangoon and was very much tempted to apply for the course. The lectures were to be held three times a week, from 4 to 7 p.m., including on Saturdays.

I approached my boss for special permission to enable me to attend the course and asked if I could leave early for two days, as Saturdays were half days and the office used to close at 2 p.m. It was indeed very considerate and kind of my boss to allow me to leave the office early to attend the training course. I sent in my application and was very lucky to get through the interview and test. My Japanese language skills helped me a great deal to get into this new phase of my life.

Here I would like to mention that my late husband, Shri Satyendra M. Khandwala, was very supportive and helpful. He encouraged me to complete the guide training course and I was able to pass the exam with an "A" grade. The written exam covered many subjects about India, such as places of historic importance, archaeology, iconography, different dances, music, cuisine, history, dynasties, religions, languages, etc. It was indeed a very comprehensive, detailed and interesting course.

We also had practical training in explaining to tourists about the sights in Mumbai, such as the Elephanta and Kanheri caves, our city transport system, temples, etc.

After I became a tourist guide for the Government of India in

1969, I continued to work in the office during the week and on Saturday until the afternoon. Then, on Saturday afternoons, Sundays and Bank Holidays, I would go on guide assignments. The pressure to work as a guide increased, as there was lot of demand. Ultimately, I had to give up my job in the office and take up full time work as a tourist guide. We were paid on an assignment basis and it was seasonal.

From 1969 until today, I have been working as a tourist guide and, at times, as a Japanese interpreter. It has been an extremely interesting profession and a continuous learning experience – as we meet people from different countries and learn so much about their culture, religion, food habits, weather, at times their personal problems, interesting and famous sights, public transport, etc.

We who are trained and working as government-recognized Tourist Guides are unofficial ambassadors of our country and project India in a right way and to the best of our ability. I have accompanied heads of state, royalty and backpackers as well. Maybe someday I will write about my adventures as a Tourist Guide.[2]

1. The Mumbai Opera House was the only one built in India. See https://en. wikipedia.org/wiki/Royal_Opera_House_(Mumbai). Rama and her husband lived in a district nearby called Prarthna Samaj.

2. In 2017, Rama Khandwala received the Best Tourist Guide Award from Indian President Ram Nath Kovind. See https://en.wikipedia.org/wiki/Rama_Khandwala

THE RENKOJI TEMPLE IN TOKYO

$\mathcal{S}$

*T*his is the temple that houses the ashes and the remains of Netaji Subhas Chandra Bose.[1] The Hikari Kikan members have two special prayer meetings every year.[2] One is to celebrate Netaji's birthday on January 23, 1897, and the second is to commemorate his (supposed) death anniversary of August 18, 1945.

During my visits to Japan, I had the pleasure of visiting the Renkoji Temple in Suginam, Tokyo twice. One occurred during the special prayer meeting on August 18.

Rama pays homage to Netaji's relics at Renkoji Temple, Sugimani, Tokyo, July 1988.

The Hikari Kikan members want the Government of India to take the ashes and remains of Netaji to India and build a huge and elaborate national museum, either in Delhi or in Calcutta. Our Prime Minister, Shri Narendra Modi, needs to be congratulated for his courageous and sincere efforts in declassifying some of the files on Netaji to bring out the truth about his death and the mystery surrounding it (see Appendix One and Two).

Now our Prime Minister is in consultation with Netaji's family and daughter, Anita, who lives in Munich, to establish the facts, move the ashes and build a national museum, as befitting this great and dynamic leader of our country. Subhas Chandra Bose deserves the greatest honor for his sacrifice and patriotism as the leader of the Provisional Government of Azad Hind Fauj.

Are we an ungrateful nation? Those of us who belong to the older generation have a strong feeling that Netaji has been deliberately ignored and not given his due for his brave efforts to win his country's freedom from the British. The younger generations are perhaps not even aware of his name. The proof of that came a few years ago when few of them visited the cinemas to watch the film on Netaji's life entitled *The Forgotten Hero*, directed by our most conscientious and quality-oriented director, Shyam Benegal.[3]

---

1. Several Indian leaders have visited the temple over the years to pay homage to Bose. See http://templesofjapan.com/Renkoji-Temple.html
2. The Hikari Kikan was the Japanese-run liaison office that worked with the INA during the war. See https://en.wikipedia.org/wiki/Hikari_Kikan
3. The film also received criticism from Netaji supporters who don't believe that he secretly married Emilie Schenkl in 1937 or died in the 1945 plane crash. For more details, see https://en.wikipedia.org/wiki/Netaji_Subhas_Chandra_Bose:_The_Forgotten_Hero

APPENDIX ONE: DID NETAJI DIE IN 1945?

Netaji's death in the 1945 air crash has been disputed by many scrupulous researchers and writers in voluminous Bengali books such as *Netaji Agyat Adhyay*, Vols. I and II, by Dr. Sushant Kumar Mitra, published in 1995 and 2000 respectively, and *Subhas Darpane Biswarup*, Vols. I and II, by Debesh Chandra Roy published in 2002, Prof. Samar Guha's English book, *Netaji Dead or Alive*, published in 1978, and the work of many other painstaking researchers, including Dr. Purabi Roy.[1]

As time goes by, these assertions that Netaji is still alive have become outdated. But the concocted story of his death in the air crash, fabricated for his safe escape, continues to be disputed due to political reasons at national and international levels.

The Mukherji Inquiry Commission in 2005 was asked to find out the facts about the following issues:[2]

(a) if he is dead, whether he died in the plane crash, as alleged;

(b) whether the ashes in the Japanese temple are the ashes of Netaji;

(c) whether he has died in any other manner at any other place, and if so, when and how;

(d) if he is alive, his whereabouts.

The conclusion of the Commission is as follows:

"In view of the evidences, arguments, witnesses placed before the Commission, the Commission arrived at the following conclusion:

(a) Netaji Subhas Chandra is dead; he did not die in the plane crash as alleged;

(b) The ashes in the Japanese temple are not of Netaji;

(c) In the absence of any clinching evidence a positive answer cannot be given and

(d) Answer already given in (a) above."

The outright rejection of the Mukherji Inquiry Commission Report (after its six years of intensive investigations made without bias) by the Congress Party-led U.P.A. Government of India, without any argument supporting the views discussed in the Parliament, is glaring proof of political malefaction. Some of the INA members firmly believe that Netaji escaped from Southeast Asia immediately after the surrender of Japan on August 15, 1945, with the definite aim of continuing his struggle with Russian help and co-operation.

His most trusted I.N.A. officer, Col. Habibur Rehman, had to play a double role to help him in his venture.[3] On the one hand, he pretended to turn traitor to Netaji by secretly joining the Allied forces and pretending to help them to do away with Netaji in an air crash with the help of the vanquished Japanese Army. On the other hand, he remained faithful and loyal to Netaji by helping him escape. He did that by taking the risk of burning his hand and parts of his body to confirm the story of Netaji's death in the air crash.

After their surrender on September 2, 1945, the Japanese were bound to do what the victors wanted to get done. But it is possible that they also remained faithful to their allegiance to Netaji and helped his escape with the concocted air crash story while sending him off to Russian territories safely. They could have arranged for the news of his alleged death on August 18, 1945, to be announced by the Tokyo News Agency on August 23, 1945, after the confirmation of Netaji having reached Russia safely.

Netaji is said to have died of severe burn injuries in the air crash, leading to heart failure at a Japanese Military Hospital at Taihoku (Taipei, in Taiwan) on the night of August 18/19, 1945. Different times of his death are stated by the same or different persons on different occasions. The news of death was announced by Tokyo Radio (not by the Japanese Government), five days later, stating that his body had been flown to Tokyo from Taipei.

The discrepancies in the time of death and the place of cremation in the news broadcasts, as well as statements of the persons concerned, created doubt about the truth of Netaji's alleged death. None of the Indian leaders — Gandhiji, Malviyaji, Abul Kalam Azad, Nehruji or members of the Netaji's family and his followers — believed the news to be authentic, although some changed their views later for their personal or political reasons.

The All India Congress Committee did not adopt an obituary resolution on the basis of the alleged news. Gandhiji even wrote to his family members in Calcutta not to perform his "Shraddh" on January 2, 1946. Gandhiji publicly said, "I believe Netaji is alive and is hiding somewhere." Even after meeting Habibur Rehman, who showed him his burnt hands, he was not convinced of the death report and continued to say, "It was camouflage."

The Viceroy of India also did not believe in the Tokyo news broadcasts, as revealed from the entries in his diary of those days. The Government of Japan did not officially confirm the news of Netaji's death in 1945.

The following four separate, on-the-spot, inquiries in Taihoku conducted immediately after the reported news of the alleged air crash death of Netaji also lead to disbelief. The reports were from

(1) General MacArthur of the U.S. Pacific Army, (2) Adm. Mountbatten, Chief of the Southeast Asian Allied Army, (3) British Global Counter Intelligence Combined Services and (4) the mayor of Taihoku.

All the above agencies had submitted their reports in 1945, but they were never published. Even the Government of the Free India, after Independence on August 15, 1947, remained apathetic in this regard. Despite the eagerness of all patriotic Indians to know about the disappearance, whereabouts or the alleged death of their beloved leader Netaji, this sensitive national issue was suppressed and kept in oblivion by the Nehru Government, then dominated by Mountbatten, and it continued as a permanent policy of the Government of India.

At the beginning of 1956, the Calcutta Citizen's Forum established a non-governmental Inquiry Committee with Dr. Radha Binode Pal, the well-known jurist and ex-judge of the Tokyo War Criminal's Trials, as its Chairman. That prompted Pt. Nehru, the then-Prime Minister of India, to immediately form an official inquiry committee to counteract the non-governmental Inquiry Committee headed by Dr. Radha Binode Pal.

The official committee, under the chairmanship of Shah Nawaz Khan and with Shri S.N. Moitra, I.C.S. and Shri Suresh Chandra Bose, Netaji's brother, as members, was denied any judicial power and was not allowed by Pt. Nehru to visit Taihoku in Taiwan for an on-the-spot investigation. So, it was crippled and made to prepare the report as desired by Nehruji, who also went to the extent of making an unethical statement in the parliament, while the Shah Nawaz Inquiry was still in process, saying, "the fact of Netaji Subhas Chandra Bose's death is, I think, settled beyond doubt."

The eagerness of the people to know about their self-sacrificing leader remained suppressed throughout Nehruji's life and was maintained by the highest level of the Indian administration.

It is worth noting that, since 1939, Nehruji had become a

staunch rival of Subhas Chandra Bose in every sphere of political activity, which continued with his unholy alliance with Mountbatten. This will be more vividly clear in noting the following facts. Since the time Netaji took command of the INA, Nehruji publicly condemned Netaji's idea of armed struggles against British Imperialism from outside the country, saying that he would resist Netaji from entering India with his INA forces at all costs.

On receiving a letter from Netaji written from Russia in November/December 1945 expressing his desire to return to India, Nehruji wrote to British Prime Minister Attlee, "Subhas Chandra Bose, your war criminal, has been allowed to enter Russian Territory by Stalin. This is clear treachery and betrayal of faith by the Russians, ally of the British and Americans. Please take note and do what you consider proper and fit."

Nehruji's close senior colleague, Sardar Patel, then demolished the temporary (Kutcha) cemetery of INA soldiers of Kohima. The Nehru Government, in a secret circular, prohibited the display of Netaji's photographs and disallowed any discussion about him in all the defense establishments of the country.

Smt. Indira Gandhi, Nehruji's daughter, on becoming Prime Minister of India, in response to a joint memorandum submitted by the majority of the members of parliament demanding a fresh judicial inquiry, appointed the one-man Inquiry Committee with Justice, G.D. Khosla as its Chairman, in 1971. That report turned out to be full of improprieties and discrepancies and unethical aberrations.

To pacify the agitated people, Khosla had to apologize before the Calcutta Court for derogatory remarks he made against Netaji in his report. Thus, the report lost its credibility and was severely criticized in the parliament because Justice Khosla had refused to accept the report of the immediate on-the-spot inquiry made by the mayor of Taihoku in 1945, which was more authentic.

The Khosla report was adopted by the parliament during the

Emergency period of Smt. Indira Gandhi's Government period, as most of the opposition members were then in detention.

Morarji Desai, during his Prime Ministership, revived the issue of the inquiry about Netaji's disappearance and alleged death. In a statement in the Lok Sabha on September 3, 1978, he declared: "Reasonable doubts have been cast on the correctness of the findings reached in the two reports on the basis of various important contractions in the testimony of the witnesses have been noticed. Some further contemporary records have also been made available. In the light of these records, the Government finds it difficult to accept those earlier conclusions as decisive."

But since the Morarji Government soon fell, the succeeding government did not take any interest in the matter and the issue again went into oblivion. In 1991, the issue was raised again by the then-President of India, Shri R. Venkataraman, who wrote to his contemporary. Prime Minister Shri V.P. Singh, to take up the matter. In response, Shri. V.P. Singh asked his Minister of External Affairs, Shri I. K. Gujral, to proceed with the matter, but unfortunately Singh's government also soon had to quit.

The President, Shri. R. Venkataraman, renewed the matter with the succeeding prime minister, Shri Chandra Shekhar, who wrote on March 26, 1991, "The Ministry has already started follow-up action regarding a high level investigation into the secret documents on the disappearance of Netaji Subhas Chandra Bose." But his government also changed prematurely.

The President, Shri R. Venkataraman, then twice requested the subsequent Prime Minister, Shri P.V. Narashima Rao, to pursue the matter of Netaji's inquiry. But instead of finding facts, he seems to have remained ill-informed with the events related to Netaji.

Probably to pacify the people eager to attach due importance and recognition to Netaji, he decided to confer "Bharat Ratna" on Netaji with the word "Posthumously" against his name in the citation while the question of his death was still unsolved and a case was still pending in the supreme court. That led to the rejection of the "Bharat Ratna" by the people in general and his kith and kin in particular.[4]

On the request in writing made by Justice Mukherji, the chairman of the last Inquiry Commission, on February 1, 2005, seeking all the entries of the cremation in the old register of the crematorium of Taihoku city during the period between 18 and 24 August 1945, the copies received from the Ministry of Foreign Affairs of Taiwan revealed there was no entry in the name of Subhas Chandra Bose/Chandra Bose/Netaji at all. Nor was there any entry in the name of those who were said to have died in the same air crash with Netaji during any of the dates from August 18 to 27, 1945.

Even if it is assumed that Netaji's body was flown to Tokyo for cremation, the bodies of his Japanese co-passengers must definitely have been cremated in Taiwan. The absence of the entries of any of the victims of the said air crash in Taihoku is a clear proof against the veracity of that story.

The minutes of an October 25, 1945, meeting of the India and Burma Committee of the British Cabinet, presided over by the British Prime Minister Attlee, stated: "It was generally agreed that the only civilian renegade of importance was Subhas Chandra Bose." This indicates that the British Cabinet, up until then, did not believe the death report of Netaji on the basis of the on-the-spot inquiries conducted immediately after the said air crash.

Also, it is not has not been proven that the ashes at Renkoji Temple in Suginami near Tokyo are the ashes of Netaji. A DNA test of the said ashes is impossible, according to experts of Germany, the U.K., Japan and, in India, the Hyderabad Centre of Cellular and Molecular Biology and the Centre for DNA Finger Printing and Diagnostics. The ashes of the bones and the teeth, having received high heat, made them unfit for a DNA test.

If less charred bones could be obtained in a reliably sealed plastic bag at room temperature, then the required DNA test could be conducted. But the chief priest of the Renkoji Temple did not respond to the request of the Mukherji Commission to collect the potentially less charred bone pieces from the sealed casket.

One more noteworthy fact is that even Shri Tarakeshwar Pal, the senior counsel appearing for the Government of India, conscientiously submitted that, "There were glaring discrepancies in the evidences adduced regarding the accident, as also the date and time of death, news of death and the death certificate of Netaji."

Mr. E. Bhaskaran had worked with Rash Behari Bose as his personal staff in the Indian Independence League. He was introduced by the latter to Netaji, on his arrival in Southeast Asia, as a person of the highest integrity, and was fortunate enough to remain in close association with him, working as his Confidential Secretary throughout the period of his stay in Southeast Asia. He had to bid a tearful adieu to Netaji when the latter left Bangkok in a small aircraft on August 17, 1945. In a memorial published by South Madras Cultural Association, Chennai, on the occasion of Netaji's Birth Centenary (1897-1997), E. Bhaskaran stated unequivocally:

> On the morning of August 17, 1945, Netaji and seven members of his staff left Bangkok for Saigon. Before leaving Bangkok, after all his staff got into the plane, Netaji came to meet Lt. Manwati Arya and neither of them could speak a word and just walked away to the plane. It was pre-arranged that he would go to Russia, as negotiations to that effect were conducted with the Russians through the Japanese Embassy in Moscow.
>
> But the situation changed when the Russians entered the war against Japan. So, at Bangkok, it was agreed that the Japanese would carry him to a place where a Japanese plane could land safely in Manchuria and thereafter it was Netaji's responsibility. The Japanese never wanted to take anybody except Netaji himself for various reasons.

Coming to the departure from Saigon, I am firmly of the opinion that there never was an accident in Taipei as reported by Domei News Agency and, if there was one, Netaji was not in that plane. But then what happened to him, how and where did he die, remains a mystery. We shall continue to celebrate his birthday year after year and there shall not be any death anniversary.

On the 17th morning at 4:00 a.m., he (Netaji) wrote a long letter to Thivy[5] in which he said, among other things. that he was on the eve of taking a long journey by air and, who knows, an accident may over take him. I believe even today that the accident story was planned before his departure from Bangkok."

Col. Habib Rehman, who was in a very high position in the Azad Hind Fauj, accompanied Netaji Subhas Chandra Bose and others in the same airplane going to Tokyo. Col. Habib Rehman himself narrated to me (Lt. Rama Khandwala) that the airplane had engine problems and it crashed. Netaji was seated on the front seats near the engine and was burnt very badly.

Col. Habib Rehman said his own hands were burnt. He showed me the scars. He said he tried to help Netaji but could not save him. It was the saddest moment of his life.

Rehman said that even in that painful state, Netaji commanded him to go and help the other co-passengers instead. This shows Netaji's bravery and valor up to the last moment of his life. Because of all the controversies and politics, unfortunately, Netaji's death anniversary goes unnoticed in historical dates of the Indian freedom struggle.

---

1. Roy, for example, has argued that Netaji escaped to Russia after the war. See http://www.millenniumpost.in/netaji-traced-upto-1956-in-russian-archives-says-purabi-roy-110359

2. For more on the commission, see https://en.wikipedia.org/wiki/Death_of_Subhas_Chandra_Bose
3. For more on Rehman, see https://en.wikipedia.org/wiki/Habib_ur_Rahman_(Indian_National_Army_officer)
4. The Bharat Ratna is the highest civilian award the government of India can bestow. See https://en.wikipedia.org/wiki/Bharat_Ratna
5. For more on John Thivy, see https://en.wikipedia.org/wiki/John_Thivy

APPENDIX TWO: THE MYSTERY OF NETAJI'S DISAPPEARANCE

From Dr. Purabi Roy:

Finally, in Saigon, on August 17, 1945, a meeting was held in the house of Narain Das, the former local I.I.L. (Indian Independence League) chief. The Intelligence Bureau reported the following after the meeting: "Incidentally, we have not been able to get anything on the conference between Bose and certain Japanese officers in the house of one Narain Das."

After this, there was the unbelievable announcement of his death in an air crash on August 19, 1945, at Taipei. The news reached India on August 24. Immediately after this news broke, the British started searching and examining all the necessary records left by the Japanese agency Hikari Kikan in their various East Asian offices. After a long search the British only found one record, which had very few details:

Copy
    Seatic section, 1A Unit
    7 Ind Div ALF SIAM

24 Sept (1945)

Subject: Translation of message re death of Bose found in a file of reports belonging to the H. Kikan.

1.HIKARI KIKAN SIGNAL RE: T

18 August Urgent to Secret

To: OC HIKARI KIKAN

From: Chief of Staff, Southern Army

Southern Army Signal 393

Today at 17:00 hrs (17 August), "T," with Lt. Gen. SHIDEI and others left here for Tokyo via Formosa and Datren. Inform Indian community of this. Depending on circumstances, I expect to return in two or three days.

2.To: OC KIKAN

From: Chief of Staff, Southern Army

Southern Army Signal 66 – 20 August, 1945

"T," while on his way to the capital, as a result of an accident to his aircraft at TAIHOKU at 14:00 hrs on the 18th, was seriously injured and died at midnight on the same date. His body has been flown to Tokyo by the Formosa Army.

I have thanked the Formosa Army for their kindness. Further, I have asked that proof of his death in the plane accident – remains, photographs, etc., be collected. As for the centre, I am getting staff officer TADA, who leaves Saigon on the 20th, to take up an appointment to provide them with a detailed report. I wish secrecy to be maintained in handling the matter.

3.HIKARI KIKAN SIGNAL RE: "T"

24 August, 1945

To:OC Malay Branch (TN: I no-clear) OC Saigon Embarkation Point Chief of Staff, Southern Army

From: OC HIKARI KIKAN

Re death of "T" please ensure that Indian communities are informed of the DOMEI dispatch regarding "T's" death

4.HIKARI Message 1020
27 August, 1945
To: CHIEF OF STAFF, Southern Army
From: OC HIKARI KIKAN
Request urgently the report on the later progress of
Col. HABIB RAHMAN"

After recovering Hikari Kikan's information, the British made a thorough investigative report, which includes seeing that all the records had been destroyed both at Saigon and Bangkok, except that in Bangkok a file containing the above messages was recovered. It may be that this file had been deliberately left there for the British and constituted part of the deception plan. It is rather hard to say conclusively, although all sources, both Japanese and Indian, were emphatic that Bose was dead.

Bose took with him four iron boxes of gold, probably 50 lbs in weight. While making his farewells in Bangkok, he indicated that he was not likely to return to that part of the world. All this suggests that he wanted to go underground and the Japanese had undertaken to give him the necessary protection to do so.

A source stated that after his retreat from Rangoon, Bose believed that he ought to start on a new road to Delhi.

In November and December, 1945, meetings were held in Rangoon where INA members formed the majority of the audience. In one meeting, a chair was left empty for the "Spirit of Bose" and in another the "Spirit of Bose" was appointed chairman. The meeting continued amid shouts of the usual INA slogans and the speeches appear to have been along extreme INA lines.

On December 31, 1945, *National Herald* in Delhi reported that Subhas Chandra Bose was in Russia. In response to this, the Soviet daily *Pravda* published an article entitled "About an Indian Comedian" by D. Zaslavzky.

The British referred back to their Foreign Office from Moscow in January 1946 with these comments:

Important

Pravda of 7th January contains a half column article by 'Zaslavzky' referring with heavy sarcasm to an article in the Delhi *National Herald* of December 31, 1945. This newspaper, apparently on the basis of information received from their Lahore correspondent, who is stated to have stayed with an 'Unnamed Soldier,' relates that Subhas Chandra Bose has fled to Russia ...

This Fascist, according to the Indian newspaper, is free to travel around the Soviet Union and inspect his army of 30,000 men and have talks with responsible representatives of the Soviet Government, who have given him 'Concrete assurances.' Information from the Indian newspaper occupies one quarter of the space in the article and the remainder consists of labored refutations of the report and accusations against the Indian Newspaper of conducting an anti-Soviet 'lying campaign.'

In early 1946, differing information was available relating to the alleged death of Netaji. The results were not entirely satisfactory because of many discrepancies. Until clarified, it would be difficult to arrive at any definite conclusion.

Major Toye's confidential comments on the subject, "Death of Bose," in CS. D.I.C. report: "What is concerning us most immediately is the information which is coming in indicating that there is a growing belief in India that Bose is alive ... statements to the same effect are being made in this country, and elsewhere."

Major Toye further states: "It seems clear that Bose and his staff were trying to make a getaway to Russia... Gandhi stated publicly at the beginning of January that he believed that Bose was alive and in hiding.

There is, however, a secret report which says that Nehru received a letter from Bose saying he was in Russia. The information alleged that Gandhi and Sarat Bose are among those who are aware of this ... In January also, Sarat Bose is reported to have said that he was convinced that his brother was alive."

In the same report he writes: "The Governor of the Afghan province of Khost has been informed by the Russian Ambassador in Kabul that there were many Congress refugees in Moscow and Bose was included in their number. There is little reason for such persons to bring Bose into fabricated stories. At the same time. the view that Bose is in Moscow is supplied in a report received from Teheran. This states that Moradoof, the Russian Vice Counsel General, disclosed in March that Bose was in Russia where he was secretly organizing a group of Russians and Indians to work on the same lines as the INA for the freedom of India."

The rumors were rife that Subhas Chandra Bose was in Russia. Finally at the request of the Director of Intelligence Branch (DIB), the Indian Political Intelligence (IPI) submitted the following note to the Indian Office with 2227 vol (8) 115/24 POI (5):

May 2, 1946
India Office : Miss Hanchet:
The Director of Intelligence Branch (D.I.B.) during his recent visit to London mentioned the receipt from various places in India of information to the effect that Subhas Chandra Bose was alive in Russia. In some cases, circumstantial details have been added."

The enigma compelled the British to put an end to this controversy. It made them prepare a final death report. But unfortunately, there were two death reports. Some insight may be gleaned from these reports. The death reports contain inherent discrepancies and conflicting statements from two different doctors who claimed to have treated Bose in a hospital on August 18, 1945.

First, a report by the office of the military adviser

attached to the United Kingdom Liaison Mission in Japan, British Embassy, Tokyo. Drafted by Lieutenant Colonel J.G. Figges on July 25, 1946, it said: 'A very thorough investigation has been conducted in Tokyo to establish the precise details of the circumstances surrounding the reported death of Subhas Chandra Bose.

Sub-Lieutenant (Medical) Tsuruta had issued a certificate showing 'death due to heart failure resulting from multiple burns and shock.'

'As a result of a series of interrogation of individuals... it is confirmed as certain that S.C. Bose died in a Taihoku Military Hospital (Nammon Ward) sometime between 19 hours and 20 hours local time on August 18, 1945.'

What may act as a supplement to the Figgess Report is the statement by Dr. Yoshimi Taniyoshi, a Medical Officer of Japanese Imperial Army, who claimed to have treated Bose under his supervision. The statement was received originally from the war crimes liaison officer, Hong Kong, when Dr. Yoshimi Taniyoshi was interned at the Staneley Gaol on October 19, 1946. According to Yoshimi's statement, Bose died at about 23 hrs.

Regarding the death certificate, Dr. Tsururta said that he had issued one, as mentioned in the Figges report, where as in the MI-2 report, a second death certificate was issued by Dr. Yoshimi where he says, 'Therefore made out a death certificate, stating the cause of death to be extensive burning and shock.'"

The issue appears more puzzling when we look into the KGB dossier that contains information following the Japanese capitulation in the first half of September 1945. During the war period from 1942 onward, a Soviet agent named V.G. Sayadiyants was living in Bombay and was engaged in selling Soviet periodicals, literature and records. He had regular contact with members and activists of the Communist Party of India.

In August 1946, J. Nehru requested that Sayadiyants deliver a letter from him personally to Comrade Stalin. Sayadiyants, on his way to Moscow via Teheran, left a note of his political observations about India for Soviet Ambassador Sadchikow in Iran. The report, dated Teheran, September 1, 1946, is entitled, "A brief survey of the political situation in India." where he suggested which party or organization would be appropriate to take charge after India's Independence.

Sayadiyants said that the Congress Party had the strongest mass base. The public in general worshipped Gandhi as a religious figure and had fantastic love for him and had faith in Nehru. The party had very solid financial support from the big industry houses like Tata, Birla, Bajaj, the textile magnets and from other capitalists.

His next review was of the Communist Party of India (CPI). Comrade Somnath Lahiri, a member of the central committee of the CPI, made a short trip to the USSR from July 23 to August 3, 1946. Lahiri felt that both Congress and the League had adopted a defeatist attitude by joining hands with the British Imperialism.

His third investigative report is about Forward Bloc. He gave a long, detailed account of the formation, development and activities of Forward Bloc. According to Sayadiyants, Forward Bloc is not a party but a platform founded by Subhas Chandra Bose that attracted thousands of followers, beyond the present 100,000 membership.

One feels curious to know what message was in the secret letter that Nehru asked Sayadiyants to deliver to Stalin. What made the Soviet agent indicate in his political note that Forward Bloc could be considered the only alternative organization after India's Independence? Did he try to indicate something more?

Many conjectures, speculations, and incoherent reports

prevailed on the issue of Bose's death. An inquiry committee (1956) and later on an inquiry commission (1972) were set up but none of these attempts could satisfy the public with conclusive proof.

The inquiry would have remained unchallenged if not for Lord Peter Archer of the Labour Party in the British Parliament, who persuaded the British Government to declassify a few war office records of M-12 at the Public Record Offices in London related to Subhas Chandra Bose, the Indian Freedom struggle, the role of the Indian National Army, and Bose's relations with the USSR and Germany.

Throughout the Soviet period in Russia, scholars were either ignorant or deliberately remained silent on this matter. Then "Glasnost" and "Perestroika" melted the seventy year iceberg in the Soviet archives to make accessible many documents related to Subhas Chandra Bose and Comintern, the Soviet TASS agency and many interesting documents have yielded new lines of research. At present, Russian scholars and researchers are showing immense interest in this subject, which might help to throw more light on unknown facts.

Following this, the Government of India took a revolutionary step to declassify around one thousand files on the Indian National Army and Netaji Subhas Chandra Bose. In 1996. a Parliamentary delegation from India went to Moscow that included Shri Chitta Basu, the Forward Bloc All India General Secretary. One document from the GRU (Military Intelligence) in the Russian Federation archive was handed over by Alexander Koleshikov to Shri Basu. The document indicates the presence of Netaji Subhas Chandra Bose in Russia, in October 1946. In the document, the Kremlin leaders, e.g. Stalin, Mototov, Voroshilov and Malik, are discussing Chandra Bose's stay in the U.S.S.R.

This particular note was handed over by Koleshikov to Shri Chitta Basu on the premises of the President Hotel in Moscow. Unfortunately, after his (Chitta Basu's) return from Russia, he remained silent and later died. But another member of the Forward Bloc, Shri Jayanta Roy, was also a delegate. While being examined by Justice M. Mukherji's Enquiry Commission, Jayanta Roy admitted that the document had been handed over to Shri Chitta Basu in his presence.

APPENDIX THREE: AZAD HIND PROCLAMATION

Proclamation of the Provisional Government of Azad Hind, October 1943:

After their first defeat at the hands of the British in 1757 in Bengal, the Indian people fought an uninterrupted series of hard and bitter battles over a stretch of one hundred years. The history of this period teems with examples of unparalleled heroism and self-sacrifice. And, in the pages of that history, the names of Siraj-ud-Daulah and Mohanlal of Bengal, Haider Ali, Tipu Sultan and Velu Tasupi of South India, Appa Sahib Bhonsle and Peshwa Baji Rao of Maharashtra, the Begums of Oudh, Sardar Shyam Singh Arariwala of Punjab and, last but not least, Rani Laxmibai of Jhansi, Tantia Tope, Maharaja Kunwar Singh of Dumraon and Nana Sahib among others – the names of all those warriors are forever engraved in letters of gold.

Unfortunately for us, our forefathers did not realize at first that the British constituted a grave threat to all of India, and therefore they did not put up a united front against the enemy. Ultimately, when the Indian people were roused to the reality of the situation, they made a concerted move and under the flag of

Bahadur Shah in 1859, they fought their last war as free men. In spite of a series of brilliant victories in the early stages of this war, ill-luck and faulty leadership gradually brought about their final collapse and subjugation. Nevertheless, such heroes as the Rani of Jhansi, Tantia Tope, Kunwar Singh and Nana Sahib live like eternal stars in the nation's memory to inspire us to greater deeds of sacrifice and valor.

Forcibly disarmed by the British after 1859 and subjected to error and brutality, the Indian people lay prostrate for a while, but with the birth of the Indian National Congress in 1885, there came a new awakening. From 1885 until the end of the last World War, the Indian people in their endeavor to recover their lost liberty tried all possible methods, namely agitation and propaganda, boycott of British Goods, terrorism and sabotage and finally armed revolution. But all these efforts failed at that time. Ultimately in 1920, when the Indian people, haunted by a sense of failure, were groping for a new method, Mahatma Gandhi came forward with a new weapon of non-cooperation and civil disobedience.

For two decades thereafter, the Indian people went through a phase of intense patriotic activity. The message of freedom was carried to every Indian home through personal examples, people were taught to suffer, to sacrifice, and to die in the cause of freedom. From the centre to the remotest villages, people were knit together into one political organization. Thus, the Indian people not only recovered their political consciousness but became a political entity once again. They could now speak with one voice and strive with one will for one common goal.

From 1937 to 1939, through the work of the Congress Ministries, in eight provinces, they gave proof of their readiness and their capacity to administer their own affairs.

Thus on the eve of the second World War, the stage was set for the final struggle for India's liberation. During the course of this war, Germany with the help of her allies, has dealt shattering blows to our enemy in Europe while Japan, with the help of allies, has inflicted a knockout blow to our enemy in East Asia. Favored by a most happy combination of circumstances, the Indian people today have a wonderful opportunity for achieving their national emancipation.

For the first time in history, Indians abroad have also been politically aroused and united in one organization. They are not only thinking and feeling in tune with their countrymen at home, but are also marching in step with them, along the path to freedom. In East Asia, in particular, over two million Indians are now organized as one solid phalanx, inspired by the slogan of "Total Mobilization." And in front of them stand the ranks of India's Army of Liberation, with the slogan "Onward to Delhi" on their lips.

Having goaded Indians to desperation by its hypocrisy and having driven them to starvation and death by plunder and loot, British rule in India has lost the goodwill of the Indian people altogether and is now living a precarious existence. It needs but a flame to destroy the last vestige of that unhappy rule. To light that flame is the task of India's Army of Liberation. Assured of the enthusiastic support of the civil population at home and also a large section of Britain's India Army, and backed by gallant and invincible allies abroad, but relying in the first instance on its own strength, India's Army of Liberation is confident of fulfilling its historic role.

Now that the beacon of freedom is at hand, it is the duty of the Indian people to set up a provisional Government of their own, and launch the last struggle under the banner of that Government. But with all the Indian leaders in prison and the people at home totally disarmed, it is not possible to set up a provisional Government within India or to launch an armed struggle under the aegis of that Government. It is therefore the duty of the Indian Independence League supported by all patriotic Indians at home and abroad to undertake this task – the task of setting up a provisional Government of Azad Hind and of conducting the last fight for freedom, with the help of the Army of Liberation that is the Azad Hind Fauj organized by the League.

Having been constituted as the Provisional Government of Azad Hind by the Indian Independence League in East Asia, we enter upon our duties with a full sense of responsibility that has developed on us. We pray that providence may bless our work and our struggle for the emancipation of our mother land. And we hereby pledge our lives and the lives of comrades in arms to the cause of her freedom, of her welfare and the exaltation among the nations of the world.

It will be the task of the Provisional Government to launch and to conduct the struggle that will bring about the expulsion of the British and their allies from the soil of India. It will then be the task of the Provisional Government to bring about the establishment of a permanent National Government of Azad Hind constituted in accordance with the will of the Indian people and enjoying their confidence. After the British and their allies are overthrown and until a permanent national government of Azad Hind is set up on Indian soil, the Provisional Government will administer the affairs of the country in trust of the Indian people.

The Provisional Government is entitled to, and hereby claims the allegiance of every Indian. It guarantees religious liberty, as well as equal rights and equal opportunities to all its citizens. It declares its firm resolve to pursue the happiness and prosperity of the whole nation and of all its parts, cherishing all the children of the nation equally and transcending all the differences cunningly fostered by an alien government in the past.

In the name of God, in the name of bygone generations who have welded the Indian people into one nation, and in the name of the dead heroes who have bequeathed to us a tradition of heroism and self sacrifices, we call upon the Indian people to rally round our banner and strike for India's freedom. We call upon them to launch the final struggle against the British and all their allies in

India and to prosecute the struggle with valor and perseverance and full faith in final victory.

Signed on Behalf of the Provisional Government of Azad Hind:
Subhas Chandra Bose – Head of the State, Prime Minister and Minister for War and Foreign Affairs
Captain Mrs. Lakshmi Swaminathan – Women's Organization
S. A. Iyer – Publicity and Propaganda
Lt. Col. A. C. Chatterjee – Finance

Representatives of the Armed Forces:
Lt. Col. Aziz
Lt. Col. N.S. Bhagat
Lt. Col. J. K. Bhonsle
Lt. Col. Gulzara Singh
Lt. Col. A.D. Logunadhan
Lt. Col. Ehsan Qadir
Lt. Col. M. Z. Kiani
Lt. Col. Shah Nawaz

A. M. Sahay – Secretary

Advisors:
Rash Behari Bose – Supreme Advisor
Karim Ghani Debnath Das
D. M. Khan A. Yellappa
J. Thivy
Sardar Ishar Singh
A. N. Sarkar – Legal Adviser
– Syonam, 21 October 1943

Army of Freedom in East Asia
The task of liberating India is ours alone. That responsibility

we shall not cast on anybody else because that would be against our national honor.

But the enemy is ruthless and desperate, and he is armed to the teeth. Against such a foe, no amount of civil disobedience or sabotage or revolutionary terrorism can be of any avail. If, therefore, we want to expel British power from India, we have to fight the enemy with his own weapons. The enemy has already drawn the sword – he must therefore be fought with the sword.

I am confident that with the help of my countrymen in East Asia, I shall be able to organize a gigantic force which will be able to sweep away British power from India. The hour has struck and every Indian must advance towards the field of battle. When the blood of freedom loving Indians begins to flow, India will attain her freedom.

(From messages to the Indian National Army in Malaya, June 29, 1943)

Netaji's last Order of the Day

The future generations of Indians who will be born, not as slaves, but as free men, because of your colossal sacrifice, will bless your names and proudly proclaim to the world that you, their forbearers, fought, and lost the battle of Manipur, Assam and Burma, but that through temporary failure you paved the way to ultimate success and glory.

– Subhas Chandra Bose – August 17, 1945.

An Army only for India's Liberty

When the Burmese Army under 32 year old Major General Aung San rebelled against the Japanese, the Japanese sought Netaji's co-operation in putting down the Burmese's rebellion. Netaji frankly declined and said that the INA would only fight for India's freedom as it was not a mercenary force. This had a salutary effect on Aung San, who directed his army not to harm the INA.

Onto Delhi - Chalo Delhi

On February 3, 1944, Netaji spent the whole day with the Subhas Regiment talking to its officers and soldiers and reviewing their parade. Bidding them a lively and enthusiastic sendoff, he said:

There, there in a distance ... beyond that river, beyond those jungles, beyond those hills, lies the promised land ... the soil from which we sprang, the land to which we will return. Hark! India is calling – India's metropolis, Delhi, is calling. Three hundred and eighty eight million of our countrymen are calling. Blood is calling to blood. We have no time to lose. Take up your arms. There in front of you is the road that our prisoners have built.

We have to march along that road. We shall carve our way through the enemy's ranks for, if God wills, we shall die a martyr's death. And in our last sleep, we shall kiss the road that brings our Army to Delhi. The road to Delhi is the road to freedom – *"Chalo Delhi."*

"Tum humko khoon deo, Mai tumko Azadi doonga!"
(You give me blood, I will give you freedom)
– Subhas Chandra Bose

India shall be Free

Brothers and sisters! A glorious chapter in the history of struggle for freedom has just come to close and, in that chapter, the sons and daughters of India in East Asia will have an undying place.

You set a shining example of patriotism and self sacrifice by pouring out men, money and material into the struggle for India's independence. I shall never forget the spontaneity and enthusiasm with which you responded to my call for Total Mobilization. You sent an unending stream of your sons and daughters to the camps to be trained as soldiers of the Azad Hind Fauj and of the Rani of Jhansi Regiment. Money and materials you poured lavishly into the war chest of the Provisional Government of Azad Hind. In short, you did your duty as true sons and daughters of India.

I regret more than you do, that your suffering and sacrifice have not born immediate fruit. But they have not gone in vain, because they have ensured the emancipation of our Motherland and will send as an undying inspiration to Indians all over the world. Posterity will bless your name and will talk with pride about your offerings at the alter of India's freedom and about your positive achievements as well.

In this unprecedented crisis in our history, I have only one word to say. Do not be depressed at our temporary failure. Be of good cheer and keep up your spirits.

Above all, never for a moment falter in your faith in India's destiny. There is no power on earth that can keep India enslaved. India shall be free and before long.

Jai Hind!

– Subhas Chandra Bose

(Message of August 16, 1945 to Indians in East Asia)

APPENDIX FOUR: NETAJI SPEECH TO THE FAUJ

Netaji's Speech to the Fauj Soldiers On July 5, 1944, in Rangoon:

The formation of the Azad Hind Fauj has been a source of extreme worry and anxiety to our enemies. They tried to ignore its existence for a time, but when the news could no longer be suppressed, their organ – the anti-India Radio at Delhi —started propaganda to the effect that Indian prisoners-of-war, under the Japanese control, had been coerced into joining the army. This propaganda could not, however, endure long, because the news began to infiltrate into India that large number of Indian civilians from all parts of East Asia were joining the Azad Hind Fauj.

The experts of the anti-India Radio had therefore to alter their tactics. They then started fresh propaganda to the effect that Indian prisoners-of-war had refused to join the Azad Hind Fauj and that, thereupon, Indian civilians were being forced into joining that Army. It did not probably strike the wise men at Delhi that if it was impossible to coerce prisoners-of-war into joining the army, it was even more impossible to coerce free civilians into becoming soldiers....

Anybody who has a grain of common sense will realize that though a mercenary army can be organized by coercion, a Volunteer Army can never be organized. You can perhaps force a man to shoulder a rifle, but you can never force him to give his life for a cause which is not his own.

At an early stage, our enemies used to say that the Azad Hind Fauj was no army, that it was merely a propaganda stunt, and that it would never fight. Later on, the anti-India Radio at Delhi began to shout that the Azad Hind Fauj had not crossed the frontier of India.

Now that the frontier has been crossed and the battle for India's freedom is being waged on Indian soil, enemy propaganda have taken recourse to a last desperate trick. They are now inventing fictitious dates supposed to have been given out by us for our entry into Delhi and are abusing us for not reaching our destination according to schedule ...

I have already told you that the Azad Hind Fauj is composed both of ex-army men as well as of ex-civilians, I may inform you further that it is composed not only of men but also of women....

Friends, the Azad Hind Fauj is the military organ of the Provisional Government and its Army are the servants of the Indian nation. Their task is to fight and liberate India. When that liberation is achieved it will be for the Indian people to determine the form of Government that they desire. The Provisional Government will then make room for a permanent Government in Free India, which will be set up in accordance with the will of the Indian people. For that glorious day we are now toiling, sweating and fighting.

APPENDIX FIVE: NETAJI ADDRESS TO GHANDIJI

Netaji's Address to Ghandiji On the Radio, July 6, 1944:

Mahatma,

After the sad demise of Shrimati Kasturba Gandhi in British custody,[1] it was natural for your countrymen to be alarmed over the state of your health ...

For Indians outside India, differences in method are like domestic differences. Ever since you sponsored the Independence Resolution at the Lahore Congress in December 1929, all members of the Indian National Congress have had one common goal before them. For Indians outside India, you are the creator of the present awakening in our country ... The high esteem in which you are held by patriotic Indians outside India and by foreign friends of India's freedom was increased a hundred-fold when you bravely sponsored the "Quit India" Resolution in August 1942.

It would be a fatal mistake on our part to make a distinction between the British Government and the British people. No doubt there is a small group of idealists in Britain – or in the U.S.A. – who would like to see India free. These idealists, who are treated by their own people as cranks, form a microscopic minority. So far as India is concerned, for all practical purposes, the British Government and the British people mean one and the same thing.

Regarding the war aims of the U.S.A., I may say that the ruling clique in Washington is now dreaming of world domination. This ruling clique and its intellectual exponents talk openly of the American Century. In this ruling clique, there are extremists who go so far as to call Britain the 49th State of the U.S.A.

I can assure you, Mahatmaji, that before I finally decided to set out on this hazardous mission, I spent days, weeks and months in careful consideration of the pros and cons of the case. After having served my people so long to the best of my ability, I have no desire to be a traitor, or to give anyone justification for calling me a traitor .... Thanks to the generosity and to the affection of my countrymen, I had obtained the highest honor which was possible for any public worker in India to achieve. I had also built up a party consisting of staunch and loyal colleagues who had implicit confidence in me.

By going abroad on a perilous quest, I was risking, not only my life and my whole future career, but what was more, the future of my party. If I had the slightest hope that without action from abroad we could win freedom, I would never have left India during a crisis. If I had any hope that within our lifetime we could get another chance – another golden opportunity – for winning freedom, as during the present war, I doubt if I could have set out from home.

There remains but one question for me to answer with regard to the Axis powers. Can it be possible that I have been deceived by them? I believe it will be universally admitted that the cleverest and most cunning politicians are to be found among the British. One who had worked with and fought British politicians all his life cannot be deceived by any other politicians in the world. If

British politicians have failed to wax or coerce me, no other politicians can succeed in doing so.

And if the British Government, at whose hands I have suffered long imprisonment, persecution and physical assault, has been unable to demoralize me, no other power can hope to do so. I have never done anything which could compromise in the least either the honor or the self respect or the interests of my country ...

There was a time when Japan was an ally of our country. I did not come to Japan so long as there was an Anglo-Japanese Alliance. I did not come to Japan so long as normal diplomatic relations remained between the two countries. It was only after Japan took what I considered to be the most momentous step in her history, namely declaration of war on Britain and America, that I decided to visit Japan of my own free will ...

Like so many of my country men, my sympathies in 1937 and 1938 were with Chungking. You may remember that as President of the Congress, I was responsible for sending out a medical mission to Chungking in December 1938.[2] Mahatmaji, you know better than anybody else how deeply suspicious the Indian people are of mere promises. I would be the last man to be influenced by Japan if her declarations of policy had been mere promises ...[3]

Mahatmaji, I should now like to say something about the Provisional Government that we have set up here. The Provisional Government has, as its one objective, the liberation of India from British rule, through an armed struggle. Once our enemies are expelled from India, and peace and order is established, the mission of the Provisional Government will be over ... The only reward that we desire for our efforts, for our suffering and for our sacrifice, is the freedom of our Motherland. There are many among us who would like to retire from the political field, once India is free ...

Nobody would be more happy than us, if by any chance, our countrymen at home should succeed in liberating themselves through their own efforts, or if, by any chance, the British Government accepts your "Quit India" resolution and gives effect to it. We are, however, proceeding on the assumption that neither of the above is possible and that an armed struggle is inevitable ... India's last war of independence has begun.

Troops of the Azad Hind Fauj are now fighting bravely in the soil of India and in spite of all difficulty and hardship they are pushing forward slowly, but steadily. This armed struggle will go on until the last Britisher is thrown out of India and until our Tri-colour National Flag proudly floats over the Viceroy's house in New Delhi.

Father of the Nation! In this holy war of India's liberation, we ask for your blessings and good wishes".

---

1. Kasturba was the wife of Mahatma Gandhi. See https://en.wikipedia.org/wiki/Kasturba_Gandhi
2. Chungking was the wartime capital of the Nationalist government in China, which was invaded by Japan in 1937. See https://en.wikipedia.org/wiki/Nationalist_government
3. Netaji's statement here should be considered in light of actual Japanese behavior in the Andaman Islands, which was ostensibly administered by Azad Hind. See https://en.wikipedia.org/wiki/Japanese_occupation_of_the_Andaman_Islands

MY GRANDFATHER, DR. PRANJIVAN
JAGJIVAN MEHTA

Before I end this book, I would like to mention that I am very proud to be the granddaughter of Dr. Pranjivan Jagjivan Mehta, who was a great friend of Mahatma Gandhi and also contributed a lot of money to the non-violence struggle of India's Independence by Mahatma Gandhi and various other institutions.

Pranjivan Mehta, grandfather of Rama Khandwala, as a student in Europe, late 1880s.

When my grandfather died on August 3, 1932, in the Rangoon General Hospital, I was only six years old and hence do not remember much about his illustrious life. It is only when I read the book *Mahatma and the Doctor* by S.R. Mehrotra[1] that I understood his very deep friendship, sacrifice and great contribution to Mahatma Gandhi and the country. He had also donated a lot of money to many deserving causes in Burma.

My grandfather was a qualified doctor, qualified lawyer and a leading jeweler in Rangoon. As one of the richest men in Burma, he was the greatest but silent philanthropist of his times.

Dr. Pranjivan J. Mehta in the late 1920s.

Gandhiji's personal tribute to Pranjivan J. Mehta, which was probably read out at the Sabarmati Ashram,[2] was contained in a letter to Narandas.[3] It reads:

If I were in Ashram now, I would have said a few words about this holy soul. He was my oldest friend. I came into contact with him when I was in England, and our relations became closer as time passed. He was the first person whom I met in England and from the beginning he acted as my guide and counselor. But all this is in the 'autobiography.' Here, I do not wish to write about our intimate relations. If we know what virtues he possessed, because of which I describe him as a holy soul, we shall be able to emulate them and can have faith that we also can achieve in our lives what he did in his.

Doctor had won a gold medal at the Grant Medical College. After that, he passed more examinations in England and was enrolled as Barrister. But I leave all these achievements. All of us cannot shine as scholars. For that, we require favorable circumstances. Men are not worshipped for their attainments in letters. It is for their virtues as firmness of mind, courage, generosity, purity, love of truth, 'ahimsa' and simplicity. Once he had made up his mind to do something, he would never change. His word therefore was trusted by people who had dealings with him. And he was always fearless. When he returned from England, he found that he could not keep up his self respect in the native town of 'Morvi,' and he, therefore, left it for good.

Doctor's liberality knew no bounds. His house was like a 'Dharamshala.' No deserving poor ever returned empty handed from him. He had helped and supported a number of people. There was no ostentation in his help. He never boasted about it. He knew no limits of caste or community or province. There were people in all provinces and belonging to all communities and faiths who have benefited from his generosity. Doctor had enough wealth to spare, but he was not proud of it. He spent very little of it on pleasure for himself. It can be said that in his very large bungalow he occupied the smallest space for his use. I don't remember him having ever spent money in self indulgence. During the last many years of his life, he loved 'brahmacharya.'

In his early life, Doctor had little interest in reading religious books, but in his later life, his love for such books increased. In a letter which he wrote to me, he mentioned the books which he had been reading. All of them were religious books. So far as I know, Doctor had scrupulously followed truth both in his business and his legal practice. I know that he had great hatred for falsehood and hypocrisy. His 'ahimsa' was visible on his face, and could be read in his eyes, and it was becoming deeper day by day. Of course the 'atman' in man never dies, but Doctor has become through his virtues, immortal in a special sense. His close connection with the Ashram was of great help in its religious aspirations. Let us learn something, each one to the best of his or her ability, from the life of this holy soul.

Not only myself, but all my family members are extremely proud of Dr. Pranjivan Jagjivan Mehta, his sacrifice and contribution to our country and the cause of non-violent struggle for Independence."

Mahatma Gandhi was great and so was my grandfather Pranjivan Jagjivan Mehta. The fighting spirit for India's freedom did not start with me. It started with my grandfather's contribution to the freedom struggle and I am proud to say that we, as a family, carried on to see India's Freedom.

(Mrs.) Rama Khandwala nee Lt. Rama Mehta

---

1. See *The Mahatma & the Doctor; The Untold Story of Dr Pranjivan Mehta, Gandhi's Greatest Friend and Benefactor, 1864-1932* by S.R. Mehrotra. Published 2014 in Mumbai by Vakils, Feffer and Simons Pvt. Ltd. The book is available in the U.S. on Amazon. Also see, https://en.wikipedia.org/wiki/Pranjivan_Mehta.
2. The Sabarmati Ashram was one of Mahatma Gandhi's residences. See https://en.wikipedia.org/wiki/Sabarmati_Ashram
3. Most likely Narandas Gandhi, a nephew of the Mahatma's and a manager at his Sabarmati Ashram.

ABOUT THE AUTHOR

Rama Khandwala nee Mehta was born in Rangoon, Burma, on December 3, 1926, the fifth of seven siblings. Her grandfather was Dr. Pranjivan Jagjivan Mehta, a prominent benefactor of Mahatma Gandhi and his struggle for India's independence.

At the age of 17, during World War II, Rama Khandwala and her sister Neelam joined the Rani of Jhansi Regiment as privates after hearing a speech by Netaji Subhas Chandra Bose in Rangoon. She was soon promoted to second lieutenant and served as a soldier and nurse during the Indian National Army's campaign in Burma. After the war, the British placed her and her family under house arrest in Rangoon for six months.

Moving with her family to Mumbai in 1946, she married Satyendra M. Khandwala in 1949. The couple had a daughter, Bina, in 1959. Her husband died in 1982.

During the postwar years, Rama Khandwala became a tourist guide with the government of India. Building on Japanese language skills learned during the war, she improved her fluency in Japanese and specialized in working with Japanese visitors to India. During one stint as an interpreter for a Japanese documentary film crew, she met the Dalai Lama and accompanied the King of Bhutan on a hike to Mumbai's Elephanta Island cave temples.

Rama being blessed by the Dalai Lama while interpreting for a Japanese television film crew making a documentary on Tibetan Buddhism.

In 2016, the Azad Hind Fauj honored her with a Life Time Achievement Award for her service in the Rani Jhansi Regiment during World War II. In 2017, Indian President Ram Nath Kovind honored her with the *Best Tourist Guide Award* at the National Tourism Awards.

Rama Khandwala receiving Best Tourist Guide Award from Indian President Ram Nath Kovind.

In 2019, she was featured in the documentary film *Elephants Do Remember*, about her wartime experiences, directed by Swati

Pandey, Viplove Rai Bhatia and Manohar Singh Bisht of Films Division. In the same year, the film was selected to be shown at the La Paz (Bolivia) international film festival.

Rama's daughter, Bina Cline (center), son-in-law, Kenneth Cline, and granddaughter, Nikki Cline Elmore, who live in the U.S.

She passed away in Mumbai on October 28, 2021, just short of her 95th birthday. She likely had been the last surviving member of the Rani of Jhansi regiment.

AZAD HIND FAUJ AWARD

On the Auspicious occasion of 119th Birth Anniversary of Netaji
Subhas Chandra Bose, Founder of Azad Hind Fauj

NETAJI SUBHAS CHANDRA BOSE

**Life Time Achievement Award for the year 2016
To Lt. Ramaben Khandwala of
Rani Jhansi Regiment for Jeevan Gaurav Puraskar.**

Azad Hind Fauj, National President

Sd/-
Shri Aba Sahib Raut
23 January 2016, Mumbai

www.ingramcontent.com/pod-product-compliance
Lightning Source LLC
Chambersburg PA
CBHW021132020426
42331CB00005B/727